俄羅斯再次崛起？

雙 頭 鷹 的 亞 太 政 策 與 戰 略 思 想

胡逢瑛 著

◆ 筆者與台北駐莫斯科代表陳俊賢大使合影。

◆ 筆者拜訪莫斯科國立國際關係學院大學MGIMO-University學術副校長Bogaturov
（中間者）；左方為該校政治學院院長A.D. Voskressenski。

◆ 筆者拜訪莫斯科國立國際關係學院大學MGIMO-University對外關係副校長A.V. Silantiev（中間者）；左方為該校政治學院院長A.D. Voskressenski。

◆ 筆者拜訪俄羅斯世界和平基金會亞洲區主任、統一團結黨智庫副總裁G.D. Toloraya。

◆ 筆者於2011年在莫斯科國立國際關係學院MGIMO-University講課。

◆ 筆者在元智大學與彭宗平校長、王立文主任、吳玉山教授以及V.L. Artemov、A.D. Voskressenski、M.A. Troitskiy三位莫斯科國立國際關係學院來訪的學者合影，2009年台俄論壇兩院簽訂雙邊合作協議。

◆ 筆者與錢復先生、王立文主任、吳非教授和A. Lukin合影。

◆ 筆者在莫斯科與莫斯科國立大學新聞系資深教授L.N. Fedotova和小女予彤合影。

◆ 筆者與莫大新聞系創系主任Yassen N. Zasursky合影，扎蘇爾斯基目前是莫大新聞系的終身榮譽主任。

◆ 筆者與莫斯科國立大學化學院系院長V.V. Lunin院士合影留念。

◆ 筆者與莫斯科駐台代表V.N. Dobrovolskiy大使以及俄羅斯世界和平基金會亞洲事務部主任G.D. Toloraya教授合影。

◆ 筆者站在紅場上的座標建築物──聖瓦西里‧布拉仁諾大教堂旁拍照留念。

Retrospective and Prospect

Chun-chieh Huang

Distinguished Professor of History,
Dean, Institute of Advanced Studies
in Humanities and Social Sciences,
National Taiwan University
Research Fellow, Academia Sinica
E-mail: cc10.huang@msa.hinet.net
Website: http://huang.cc.ntu.edu.tw
http://www.ihs.ntu.edu.tw

◆ 筆者的老師明驥教授（前文化大學俄文系主任）、中影公司總經理，與前元智大學校長詹世弘講座教授，出席台俄國際文化與學術交流論壇，由元智大學通識教學部主辦。很遺憾的是明老師現已不在世了。

◆ 筆者與台灣大學人文社會高等研究院黃俊傑院長、元智大學通識教學部主任王立文教授、教務長王佳煌教授、廣州暨南大學吳非教授以及兩位俄羅斯學者G.D. Toloraya教授 和V. L. Artemov院士合影留念。

◆ 筆者在參訪莫斯科國立國際關係學院大學政治學院時留影。

◆ 筆者在莫斯科國立國際關係學院大學國際講者紀念廊留影。

◆ IAICS-2012大會承辦者台灣元智大學，與IAICS-2013承辦者俄羅斯遠東聯邦大學聚首元智大學；董事暨編輯會議由哈爾濱工業大學宋莉會長，與羅德島大學終身教授陳國明執行長，以及ICS主編Joanna Radwanska-Williams等主持討論。

◆ 筆者與G.D.Toloraya和前政大俄羅斯研究所所長王定士教授合影留念。

◆ 筆者和女兒雨中漫步在克里姆林宮內的教堂廣場上。

◆ 筆者與指導教授──莫斯科國立國際關係學院前國際新聞教研室主任V.L. Artemov
院士合影於元智大學。

◆ 筆者與俄羅斯學者拜訪吳玉山所長。

◆ 筆者與俄羅斯學者拜訪石之瑜教授。

◆ 筆者陪同俄羅斯學者拜訪文大俄文系主任李細梅教授（右）。

◆ 筆者於2011年前往墨西哥聖里斯多博，承接2012-IAICS國際年會的承辦權。與
IAICS執行長陳國明教授（中）和主席Brooks Hill（右）於正式開幕會前合影留
念，並贈送該學會元智大學英文手冊一本。

◆ 筆者與外交部亞西司司長林進忠司長和E. Koldunova和 L.N. Fedotova兩位教授合影留念。

◆ 筆者與文化大學俄文系王愛末教授和楊景珊教授在俄文系辦合影留念。

◆ 筆者參加石之瑜老師組織的中流研習營在大陸山西大同古城上合影留念。

◆ 由陳國明教授和王立文教授指導、筆者組織策劃的2012-IAICS國際跨文化傳播學術研討會第十八屆世界年會，與會者在元智大學五館前合影留念，2013年主辦方是位於的弗拉迪沃斯克(海參崴)的俄羅斯遠東聯邦大學。

◆ 筆者與莫斯科國際關係學院大學全權事務副校長A.V. Malgin教授在亞塞拜然首都巴庫舉行的2013-MGIMO International Forum會場合影留念。

◆ 筆者與莫斯科國際關係學院大學校長Anatoly Torkunov 院士在亞塞拜然首都巴庫舉行的巴庫2013-MGIMO International Forum會場談論進行俄羅斯研究的相關問題。

ФОНД 🎯 РУССКИЙ МИР

ШЕСТАЯ АССАМБЛЕЯ РУССКОГО МИРА

исх. № 384/07

от «20» июля 2012 г.

Колонный зал Дома Союзов
Российская Федерация, Москва, ул. Большая Дмитровка, д. 1

Помощнику профессора университета Юан Жэ
г-же Фен-Юн Ху

Глубокоуважаемая госпожа Фен-Юн Ху!

Приглашаю Вас принять участие в работе VI Ассамблеи Русского мира, по традиции организуемой фондом «Русский мир» 3 ноября и приуроченной к празднованию Дня народного единства.

Главная тема предстоящей Ассамблеи – **«Русский язык и российская история».**

Русский язык как средство общения и единения народа является не просто хранителем целого пласта российской истории, но и живым пространством многомиллионного Русского мира. Сохраняя русский язык как культурный код нации, мы сможем поддерживать и приумножать важнейшие ценности и традиции, выработанные за многовековую историю России.

Указом Президента Российской Федерации 2012 год объявлен Годом российской истории. Эта идея получила активную поддержку во всем Русском мире. Мы отмечаем 1150-летие российской государственности, 400-летие освобождения Москвы от польско-литовских войск, 200-летие Отечественной войны 1812 года, а также 150-летие со дня рождения выдающегося реформатора Петра Аркадьевича Столыпина.

Ассамблея должна способствовать привлечению внимания российского общества и Русского мира к славным страницам нашей общей истории, базовым духовно-нравственным ценностям и содействовать распространению современных методик и практик популяризации русского языка и истории.

В работе Ассамблеи примут участие около тысячи российских и зарубежных представителей: высшие государственные деятели Российской Федерации; руководители министерств и ведомств, дипломатических представительств, общественных организаций, объединений соотечественников; авторитетные отечественные и иностранные ученые; российские и зарубежные преподаватели истории и славистики; известные литераторы, издатели, деятели культуры и искусства; священнослужители, активисты молодежных организаций, журналисты; видные благотворители.

Ассамблея пройдет в Колонном Зале Дома Союзов (Москва, ул. Большая Дмитровка, д.1).

Прошу Вас подтвердить Ваше намерение принять участие в Ассамблее и направить в адрес оргкомитета электронную анкету.

С уважением,

Исполнительный директор
Правления

В.А. Никонов

Приложения:
- *анкета участника Ассамблеи, которую Вы найдете по следующей Интернет-ссылке:*
  https://docs.google.com/spreadsheet/viewform?formkey=dER0NmRGYYRaUEZfaFh6UG04WmhCcUE6MQ
- *проект программы Ассамблеи*

Организаторы хотели бы особо отметить, что вход на все мероприятия Ассамблеи осуществляется только при наличии данного приглашения. Просьба иметь его с собой.

Организационный комитет VI Ассамблеи Русского мира: Т/ф.: +7(495)981-5683, +7(495)981-5682 (с 11.00 до 17.00 по московскому времени); Email: assamb2012@russkiymir.ru

◆ 筆者母校莫斯科國立國際關係學院大學MGIMO-University的校長A.V. Torkunov 發給筆者參加由亞塞拜然總統阿里耶夫在巴庫主持的MGIMO國際校友會的邀請函。Torkunov於2000年獲普京總統親自頒發國家貢獻總統勳章。

МИНИСТЕРСТВО ИНОСТРАННЫХ ДЕЛ РОССИЙСКОЙ ФЕДЕРАЦИИ
ФЕДЕРАЛЬНОЕ ГОСУДАРСТВЕННОЕ ОБРАЗОВАТЕЛЬНОЕ
БЮДЖЕТНОЕ УЧРЕЖДЕНИЕ
ВЫСШЕГО ПРОФЕССИОНАЛЬНОГО ОБРАЗОВАНИЯ
«МОСКОВСКИЙ ГОСУДАРСТВЕННЫЙ
ИНСТИТУТ МЕЖДУНАРОДНЫХ ОТНОШЕНИЙ
(УНИВЕРСИТЕТ)
МИНИСТЕРСТВА ИНОСТРАННЫХ ДЕЛ РОССИЙСКОЙ ФЕДЕРАЦИИ»

МГИМО
УНИВЕРСИТЕТ

16.01.2013   03118/01

ДОЦЕНТУ
НАЦИОНАЛЬНОГО УНИВЕРСИТЕТА ТАЙВАНЯ,
ВЫПУСКНИКУ МГИМО

ФЕНГ-ЙУНГ ХУ

Уважаемый господин Фенг-Юн Ху,

Рады пригласить Вас принять участие в I Международном форуме выпускников МГИМО (предварительная программа прилагается), который состоится 11-13 апреля 2013 года в г. Баку под патронажем Президента Азербайджанской Республики И.Г. Алиева.

Программой Форума предусмотрено проведение пленарных заседаний по следующим темам – образование, экология и энергетика, вопросы взаимодействия бизнеса и гражданского общества.

Просим по возможности сообщить о Вашем решении. Также для участия в Форуме необходимо пройти регистрацию на сайте alumniforum.mgimo.ru

Приложение: упомянутое, на 1 л.

С уважением,

РЕКТОР,   А.В. ТОРКУНОВ
ПРЕДСЕДАТЕЛЬ СОВЕТА
АССОЦИАЦИИ ВЫПУСКНИКОВ,
АКАДЕМИК РАН

R.S.V.P. +7 (495) 434-93-84, +7 (926) 929-17-69; alumni@mgimo.ru

◆ 俄羅斯國家杜馬外交委員會副主席暨俄羅斯世界和平基金會執行長V.A. Nikonov給筆者2012年第六屆大會的邀請函。

推薦序

石之瑜教授

在明明是身處全球化時代，對此還感到驕傲的台灣，卻一直仰賴英語媒體提供訊息，其中尤其是受到美國媒體主導，胡逢瑛教授此時此地出版《俄羅斯再次崛起？——雙頭鷹的亞太政策與戰略思想》一書的重要性，是顯而易見的。凡事唯美國馬首是瞻的習性，在台灣的新聞界與學術界不是祕密，然而我們已經遭遇瓶頸卻不肯面對，則不得不究責於在地文化的惰性與墮落。我們不僅僅是仰賴美國大量地輸入關於美國的資訊，更依靠美國來認識世界，甚至包括認識台灣自己。如何擺脫我們加諸於自己的英語桎梏與美國觀點，是時代賦予在地知識分子的任務。胡逢瑛教授一馬當先，值得敬佩。

台灣對俄羅斯的認識極其有限，遑論從來自俄羅斯的各種觀點認識世界或認識台灣。從俄羅斯來台執教的學人中，不少有深厚漢學基礎，然而其中與出版界深入而能進行有品質的交往者，屈指可數。從俄羅斯或斯拉夫語系所畢業後的大學生，縱使其中積極參與全球資源的匯流，並開展個人生涯有成者頗多，而後來進一步深造並愛好深度寫作的，則著實尚待培養。其結果，關於俄羅斯種種，充其量豐富了奇風異俗的旅行文學，並沒有得以在國人腦海中注入其深厚、豐富又獨特的思想淵源。對俄羅斯諸多思想視野的闕如，除了囿限我們自己的想像空間之外，更值得注意的是，也讓我們當代生活中始終息息相關的中國歷史文化，流於偏狹成見的犧牲品。

俄羅斯對中國的歷史文化有長遠而深刻的體認，尤其與歐美主流中國專家不同的是，俄羅斯思想史上的中國，敏銳而廣泛地從北疆中國向南開展，與教科書上那種隨著歐美傳教士腳步由南向北，從廣州出發，以鴉片戰爭為斷代起點的帝國主義世界史，兩者之間的差別，可以說是天南地北。俄羅斯的傳教士與歐洲的天主教及美國的基督教各有隸屬，俄人對於中國經典研究所投入的精神與挹注的資源，至今已成就了三百年以上的積累，到現在仍然是俄羅斯菁英階層藉以與中國接觸交往的認識基礎。他們關注的課題乃涵蓋了歐美漢學界不熟悉的契丹、西夏、蒙古、滿州等等，再加上地屬俄羅斯的西伯利亞，與濱臨太平洋一直到遠東的海疆，俄羅斯在歷史上便與中國之間有無法切割的地緣與親緣。

這樣的國度所醞釀的戰略思想，既有其地緣性，又有其多元性，見證在俄、中的歷史交往關係中，表現出親近性與衝突性並呈的複雜情感，前者描述了社會與人民之間的交流，後者當然間歇地成為兩國政治關係的注腳。如何從過去的文化價值與世界觀當中擷取資源，建構出當代戰略的背景，向來是俄羅斯戰略思想的特色之一，尤其是進行對華政策有關的智庫專家，無不是從語言與漢學的傳統中養成，與美國智庫藉由邏輯與數據來掌握對手的風格，可說是分庭抗禮。他們能從林語堂所論幽默，或易經所書生生不息，甚或少數民族風俗中，體會中共黨中央一言一行的深意，這應該是華府中人斷斷不會、也想不到的方法。

看到俄羅斯漢學家茹苦含辛地在俄中關係低迴的年代裡，默默地繼續關注中國經典的研讀，讓兩國文化關係的相互流通在潛層裡泛流不絕，台灣是否也能透過民間自發的動能，對似遠實近的北國，發展知識與文化上的流通，逐漸融入、容納、彼此涵化與培養？難道這不是迫在眉睫的挑戰嗎？胡逢瑛教授因緣際會地從俄羅斯留學歸國，風雲際會地目睹俄羅斯再崛起的潮流，當她幸運地進入到沒有厚重制度包袱的元智大學，再無獨有偶締結連理於來自廣州的俄羅斯專家吳非教授，可以說是已經得天獨厚地保證會在台灣的俄羅斯研究界闖出名堂。而她果然不負眾望地完成此書，這不但是對在地知識界的開示，也是對俄羅斯的獻禮，更是對大時代的報答。

目 次

俄羅斯的亞太政策

——問題與影響

2012年，普京在擔任總理四年之後再度回到俄羅斯最高權力核心的位置。普京重返克里姆林宮更大程度上影響了世界秩序的重建以及國際政治經濟的格局，俄羅斯會更好地運用國際參與的全球化戰略計畫來提高國內現代化進程的向前發展。俄羅斯民眾仍然期待普京在國家現代化進程中可以更加有效地提高民眾的生活水準與社會的生存環境。俄羅斯在穩固與獨聯體關係和歐盟關係的同時，已經將對外關係的視野轉向亞洲。俄羅斯重返亞洲的動力來自於亞洲經濟的增長與實力：金磚國家聯盟與上海合作組織加深了俄印中的合作與互動關係。俄羅斯將提高國內經濟的要素轉向了東方，俄羅斯的亞太戰略將會作為俄羅斯內部改革的主要動力來源。此間，中俄關係的發展成為俄羅斯亞太戰略的重要組成要素。俄羅斯將文化政策與經濟政策與中俄關係的發展緊密聯繫在一起，俄羅斯與中國的關係將會在戰略性與實用性的框架下加深雙邊的經濟合作，俄羅斯重返亞洲的亞太戰略將會影響中美關係以及亞太國家間的關係，包括了對台海關係的影響，可以說，俄羅斯的能源經濟戰略將會更好地與外部區域安全和內部現代化的總體經濟改革結合在一起。

一、俄羅斯現代化進程之意涵

2012年10月24日，俄羅斯經濟現代化與創新發展聯席會舉行了第一屆會議，普京總統出席了會議並且發表致詞，該跨部門部會主要是根據普京於同年6月18日簽署的總統令而正式成立的。俄羅斯現代化是一個全面的改革工程建設。普京實際上

◆ 普京總統召開跨部門會議，討論現代化工程的進程（照片來源：俄羅斯總統府官網）

是把原來總統府架構下與政府內部若干個發展委員會合併組建為一個較大的聯合部會，顯示了普京回鍋擔任總統之後的執政重點，普京啟動了今後至少在其任內六年總統期間最重要的現代化進程。

　　普京認為現代化是俄羅斯在全球經濟立足的重要基礎。俄羅斯的經濟發展需要仰賴出口多樣化並且保存內部的市場，強化內部本土產業的立基條件在於現代化的推動。普京總統對於俄羅斯現代化的思路與概念基本上是建立在如何借助和吸引大型的國內外企業，進入到俄羅斯的高等教育與科學研究院的體系當中來運作，這樣一方面可以更新現有的設備基礎、擴大研究範圍與技術革新層面，也直接培養了俄羅斯內部的人才，總體使人才養成與研究成果更為有效地投入到技術創新產業當中；另一面，企業可以獲得所需要的各種人才，為企業創新發展提供更多穩定的人才來源。但是，俄羅斯法律的不明確和官僚體制導致了國外企業沒有足夠的安全保障和限制了投資意願。俄羅斯政府必須要為國外企業建立好足夠的市場環境。因此在保存與強化內部市場上，俄羅斯政府正在努力要立法來保護投資者的智慧財產權益，給予投資者可能的優惠與保護政策，以期吸引外資投入到俄羅斯重點發展的研發產業領域當中。

俄羅斯在醫療、生化、信息、軍工、航太與核能發展都有很好的基礎，但是過去在蘇聯時期這些產業都是配合國家的軍事化產業來發展的，如何將這些產業運用到民生領域當中是產業轉型的重點。在俄羅斯國防安全戰略考慮之下，俄羅斯必須要在內部來建立自己的研究創新體系，但是國外企業投入到這些領域會受到很多的限制，俄羅斯政府則希望結合企業投資與俄羅斯既有的高等教育和研究院體系來落實現代化政策。尤其是如何吸引外資進入到教育與科學領域，這樣一來可以填補俄羅斯研究缺乏基礎設備的空間，同時也可以在提升人才與研究成果的同時，建立俄羅斯內部的運作市場，使俄羅斯未來出口不必完全依靠石油與天然氣不可再生的能源來獲取利益。俄羅斯基本上生產所有科技所需要的原材料，對於俄羅斯出口原材料加工產業、軍工產品、生化產品以及出口產業多樣化都有助益。

俄羅斯現代化與西化關係密切，通常體現兩種特點：一面是從落後到進步的激烈改革，中央權力的強化與集中；另一面則是國力強大的彰顯與對外擴張。俄羅斯在十世紀末的基輔公國時期，弗拉基米爾大公選擇東正教為國教，強迫人民受洗為東正教徒，之後俄羅斯有了兩百年歷史的強盛時期。彼得大帝西化政策之後，俄羅斯科技與教育突飛猛進，凱薩琳女皇延續了科學發展觀，俄羅斯自此強盛了三百年，十九世紀初在打敗拿破崙入侵之後成為歐洲強國。史達林的工業化政策使蘇聯成為工業強國，蘇聯打敗納粹德國之後，與美國並列為世界兩極強權。俄羅斯鮮少在政治與經濟上參照西方模式會達到國力的強盛，而是在技術運用上與自由思想方面會汲取西方的養分。普京目前完成了俄羅斯石油公司收購秋明－英國石油公司的進程，顯示俄羅斯一方面會繼續強化能源海外擴張的策略，作為穩定俄羅斯經濟增長的基礎；另一方面會全面的擴大內部現代化的工程，吸引海外資金進入俄羅斯，參與到俄羅斯現代化的工程當中，以穩定俄羅斯內部市場發展所需要的人才、技術和資金。

蘇聯解體後的十年，葉利欽總統的政策基本上是自由化與民主化，利用體制與西方接軌促使俄羅斯融入西方國家的體系當中。普京執政後，強調國家化與社會化，借由能源與媒體產業的國家化來促進經濟成長與推動社會服務政策。普京於2002年首先提出教育現代化的發展戰略目標。俄羅斯在蘇聯解體之後面臨精神與物質上的危機，普京首先利用發展訊息化工程將俄羅斯原有的國家圖書館資料電子化，讓俄羅斯傳統的文學典籍和歷史教材都能在網路上簡單取得，以此來推廣俄羅斯的經典教育，重新恢復俄羅斯經典對於俄羅斯人民素養的教化作用；其次是建立統一的教育訊息化空間，縮小區域間的教育落差，強化愛國思想教育。除此之外就是校園空間的現代化。蘇聯時期，除了莫斯科大學以外，幾乎所有的專業院校與研究院都沒有校園的規劃，目前各地方區域政府希望利用大學城的建設來吸引外資進入校園並且以此留下本地的人才。梅德維傑夫則進一步推動經濟的現代化與技術創新概念，與西方國家再度合作來進行俄羅斯現代化革新的進程。普京回鍋擔任總統後，結合國家化與國際化來持續推動俄羅斯經濟現代化的改革。普京在國際問題上採取較為獨立於美國的政策，在建立中國與美國對於亞太區域衝突問題上的緩衝空間，與亞太國家進行更多的安全與經濟利益的合作。

俄羅斯現代化進程基本牽動了俄羅斯內部資源有限以及如何分配資源的問題。俄羅斯在過去二十年當中失去了許多人才與發展人才的基礎，許多俄羅斯人到了海外之後，顯少為俄羅斯的國家發展和利益作出貢獻。當俄羅斯在近十年當中靠著能源出口為俄羅斯經濟成長帶來利潤時，俄羅斯政府希望藉由俄羅斯歷史、文化和語言來凝聚海外僑民的民族意識並且加強獨立國協國家人民對於俄羅斯的認同。為此，普京於2008年還成立了俄羅斯世界和平總統基金會來執行這項任務。但是，俄僑與前蘇聯加盟共和國的人總是會埋怨俄政府給的條件太少，前蘇聯加盟共和國的人還希望取得俄羅斯的國籍來享受俄羅斯的福利政策，這使得俄羅斯政府對於這些蘇聯解體後紛紛獨立的加盟共和國的人感到非常頭痛，因為俄羅斯已經把許多勞工市場開放給這些前蘇聯國家的民眾，主要還是中亞的國家，俄羅斯又開始為前蘇聯國家的經濟成長扮演主要的角色。俄羅斯目前需要更多的資金與技術投入到國家的現代化基礎建設當中。俄羅斯面臨的困境依然巨大，當然前景仍然不可限量。

二、從普京訪中來看俄外交之意涵

俄羅斯總統普京在2012年5月7日正式宣佈就職之後，旋即簽署總統令表示，要建立「從大西洋至太平洋」的「歐亞太」一體化空間作為俄羅斯未來外交政策的長期戰略目標。普京在闊別總統職務四年之後，又在2012年3月4日以百分之63.6的得票率當選而回鍋擔任總統，普京上任之後的一個月之內，遂迅速積極展開了他外交上的國是訪問之旅。然而，普京一開始便缺席了5月18日與19日在美國戴維營舉行的八國集團峰會，但卻在5月31日起，連續出訪了白俄羅斯、德國、法國、烏茲別克斯坦、中國和哈薩克斯坦。其中，普京於6月5日至7日訪問中國三天，停留時間最為長久，並出席在北京舉行的上海合作組織成員國元首理事會第十二次會議，與中國大陸的領導人胡錦濤、溫家寶以及習近平先後會晤。普京的國是訪問被外界解讀為未來俄羅斯外交政策的基本走向：疏美、拉歐、合中以及穩獨聯體。整體而言，普京的外交戰略特點比梅德維傑夫更強調俄羅斯對於和美國處理國際問題的不同調以及俄羅斯獨立外交的傳統風格，這也是普京重返克里姆林宮執政之路必須克服來自於莫斯科反對派勢力的崛起和美國內政干涉的一種反制作為。而訪問中國是普京建立亞洲關係以及突破西方圍堵的基礎，同樣地，中國不斷在面臨美國重返亞洲的壓力與南海問題的騷擾之後，中俄之間的關係是否會有近一步的發展也備受關注。

普京總統就任之後，並沒有馬上參加該年在美國舉行的八國集團峰會，一方面輿論認為這是普京與歐巴馬對於敘利亞制裁以及伊朗核和朝核問題不同調的矛盾結果，巧合的是美國方面也宣佈歐巴馬將不會出席9月份在海參崴（符拉迪沃斯托克）舉行的亞太經合組織會議，美俄兩國總統似乎有意在國際衝突議題上避免過早的接觸與攤牌，顯然雙方都以穩定內部問題作為首要的考量；但另一方面輿論也顯示，普京剛上任總統，對於八國集團的問題沒有時間做好充分的準備，過去四年普京在內閣擔任總理，首要的工作在於內政，主要體現在對執政黨統一團結黨內部進行控制與整合，以及加強國內安全問題與反腐改革的工作，但沒有辦法干涉梅德維傑夫總統的外交走向，而現在普京要對俄羅斯外交採取更多的協調與談判空間，不讓西方國家在經濟領域和外交領域同步控制全球的政治與軍事格局。

6月3日與4日，第29次「俄羅斯－歐盟峰會」在俄羅斯聖彼德堡舉行。俄羅斯是一個能源輸出國，而歐盟很多國家需要進口能源，如果純粹從經濟角度上來看，俄羅斯必須在全球金融與歐債危機之後將經濟視角從西方轉向東方，但是從俄羅斯對歐洲的影響和控制的長遠發展關係而言，俄羅斯屬於西方文明世界的一環，俄羅斯仍需要對歐洲國家進行紓困來維持歐俄之間的友好關係。在國際政治問題上俄羅斯與歐洲卻有先天的矛盾關係，北大西洋公約組織仍在美國的控制下對俄羅斯進行冷戰時期的圍堵。

面對來自於西方國家在地緣政治上的戰略圍堵，普京的多極化外交戰略將會全面從結合發展中國家的經濟體合作展開，例如金磚國家聯盟，亞洲有中印俄三國傳統對話的機制，再結合拉丁美洲的巴西和非洲的南非，其代表著俄羅斯以聯合全球最大的經濟體國家的聯盟策略來爭取參與國際政治並影響國際局勢的態度，並且俄羅斯將以其軍事、能源以及傳統外交的大國優勢，可以在發展中國家扮演協調和組織的角色，以平衡來自於美國或是中國對於區域控制所構成的威脅與壓力，顯然，俄羅斯在全球治理的目標中找到自己的外交定位。

蘇聯解體之後，俄羅斯在外交方面全面棄守，過去聯繫亞洲的社會主義與國際共產的意識形態因素徹底毀滅。俄羅斯版圖橫跨歐亞大陸，但是俄羅斯的國家發展和國力強大來自於受到歐洲文明和科技的影響，俄羅斯對於亞洲的認知受到過去蒙古人統治、日俄戰爭的失敗、中俄五十年代末期交惡的負面影響，以及蘇聯解體之後中亞民族對於俄羅斯經濟的逐漸依賴，大批中亞的勞工在莫斯科從事底層的苦力工作，總體而言，亞洲對於俄羅斯似乎是負面的概念居多。

普京再次回鍋擔任總統之後，首先面對的是西方國家在金融危機之後所採取的顏色革命的策略壓力。在梅德維傑夫擔任總統期間，他的外交策略傾向於與西方合作，對於阿拉伯國家發生的獨裁政權倒台多採取西方的意見，這與普京的獨立外交有一定的區別，然而普京在總理期間必須隱忍梅德維傑夫的親西方的外交態度，梅德維傑夫的現代化與自由化政策事實上養成了俄羅斯的反對派勢力，這對於普京再回克里姆林宮的道路增加了難度。然而，普京近十年以來在俄羅斯的支持度超過半數以上是無庸置疑的，因此選舉舞弊的新聞並不能夠影響普京的當選，但是從去年以來爆發的大規模示威遊行抗議活動卻足以構成普京執政的威脅和壓力。

與此同時，莫斯科的自由派如何在普京執政之後獲得發展的空間，仍是反對派勢力的抗爭目標，這樣一來，西方在金融危機之後，無法在北大西洋公約組織的軍事東擴效應下繼續圍堵俄羅斯，西方同樣面對經濟崛起的中國，人權與支持反對派的工作成為最有效且便宜的路徑。普京再任總統之後的外交會趨於保守，不會在國際地位上與中國和美國衝鋒競爭，但是在區域聯合策略上俄羅斯在國際上的影響力與協調角色將會大大增加，普京仍然會奉行多極與多邊政策，以因應美國單極主義之下和中國經濟獨霸的操控與影響。

三、俄遠東發展對中俄關係的影響

2012年9月亞太經合會議在俄羅斯遠東海參崴舉行，普京的全球治理戰略將從落實亞洲戰略開始，屆時俄羅斯將藉由此次會議的多邊與雙邊經貿談判，來提高俄羅斯遠東的經濟發展並將遠東長期發展作為俄羅斯與亞太地區經貿合作的營運區域，而海參崴將成為俄羅斯重返亞洲的重要門戶與窗口。

普京的亞洲政策將以能源作為進入亞洲市場的基礎，但是能源不是唯一的因素，與亞洲國家合理與長期有效的經貿合作關係更符合俄羅斯國家發展所需要的正常化經貿關係，尤其歐洲受到全球金融危機的與歐債的負面影響之後，俄羅斯的能源收入受到了影響，如果俄羅斯與中國能夠在能源價格方面取得更多的優勢，中俄關係將得到進一步發展。2001年中俄貿易額106億美元，2011年上升為792.4億美元，中國一躍成為俄羅斯第一大貿易夥伴。中俄兩國領導人也將「2020年達到2000億美元」作為未來十年中俄經貿關係的發展目標。

普京回鍋擔任總統之後，中俄在遠東地區的合作也值得關注。隨普京一同訪問中國的有多位內閣部長，其中包括新成立的遠東發展部部長維克托・伊沙耶夫。隨團訪問還有俄羅斯能源部會首長以及天然氣石油企業與銀行總裁，中俄之間以遠東作為經濟合作的平台成為普京亞洲新戰略的重點。過去由於遠東地區的地位敏感以及經濟發展落後，加上人口稀少，長期無法受到莫斯科的關照，再加上普京的反腐政策與打擊邊境非法貿易聯繫在一起，這引起遠東地區和中國方面的不滿。但是隨著俄羅斯能源政策以尋求亞洲市場作為未來普京落實亞洲新戰略的基礎，以及藉由亞太經合會議在俄羅斯海參崴舉行召開之際，俄羅斯需要了解中國未來領導人對於俄羅斯亞洲戰略的態度，中國是否能夠理解俄羅斯解決內部經濟犯罪問題必須得到中國在中亞地區和遠東地區關係正常化的合作，以及俄羅斯在亞太區域的經貿關係將無意挑戰中國的地位。中俄雙方需要在此問題取得互信與諒解，否則普京將對美國重返亞洲以及對中國主導重啟朝核六方會談和南海島嶼主權問題採取冷漠的態度。

中國未來新任領導人也同樣面臨來自於內部的鬥爭和美國干涉的問題。普京訪問中國可以作為瞭解中國領導層對於俄羅斯重返亞洲外交政策的態度。普京的亞洲戰略對於美國的壓力多於對中國的壓力。中國在亞太地區的任何動作都會引起美國的不滿和制裁，越南開放金蘭灣軍事基地租用引來美國在南海軍事佈局的動作，黃岩島對峙問題引起南海區域內菲律賓、越南、馬來西亞等周邊國家的恐慌以及挑戰了美國傳統安全勢力的範圍，中國在亞太地區安全問題上更加趨於孤立，經濟崛起仍然無法解決中國作為大國崛起後所需要的國際支持與信任。

中國似乎只剩下上海合作組織這個國際合作的區域聯盟平台，來平衡美國對於中國的圍堵。而上海合作組織的發展逐漸會由俄羅斯代表中亞國家與中國進行各項的合作與談判。在北約勢力逐漸淡出阿富汗之後，上合組織成員國將在中亞安全與邊境問題方面增加合作，此時普京訪問中國的重要性與中俄領導人之間的默契與互動是未來兩國合作的基礎，如果中國領導層認識到普京亞洲政策的態度，那麼俄羅斯將會與中國有更多的互動與合作，反之，俄羅斯將忽略中國，直接落實亞洲政策，與印度、越南等東南亞國家連結起來，俄羅斯儘管無意挑戰中國在亞洲的地位，但是在金磚國家策略聯盟的合作機制之下，俄羅斯將與印度以及其他國家進行更多的經濟合作來平衡中國經濟的控制，屆時中國會更加感到孤立與壓力。

俄羅斯世界和平總統基金會掌管亞洲事務部的主任格奧爾吉·托羅拉亞教授則認為，普京重返克林姆林宮之後，強調以外交政治談判取代戰爭的國際行動將成為外交主軸，與亞太地區的經貿關係利益將大於區域爭霸的動機，普京的亞洲政策將成為俄羅斯實現全球治理戰略的重要因素，尤其在2008年全球金融危機之後，中俄之間都看到了重建國際經濟秩序的機會，然而俄羅斯和中國在內部都面對著反對派的抗議聲浪，西方介入反對派的威脅也成為兩國領導人未來的執政壓力，而俄羅斯與中國之間在國際領域的合作將是穩定各自內部發展的最為關鍵的因素。預期中俄未來在聯合國安全理事會的合作力度將大大的增加，而區域之間的合作機制如上海合作組織以及金磚國家聯盟的發展將會獲得重視，成為中俄增加互動與加強聯繫的重要平台與聯繫機制。

四、俄羅斯入世對中國的影響

2008年，俄羅斯最終入世了。表面上，俄羅斯作為市場經濟體系下的自由貿易地位受到了國際的認可，實際上，俄羅斯扮演獨立國協與金磚國家聯盟之間的重要協調者的影響力已經確定成形，這與普京再度回到克里姆林宮擔任總統密切相關。普京為俄羅斯未來20年的國家戰略安全與經濟發展定下基調——更新基礎設備，提高能源產品的品質和多元化生產，引進高科技技術和設備，增強獨立國協國家的經濟凝聚力，並且繼續加強與歐盟國家的合作。作為俄羅斯的第一大交易夥伴和鄰國，這對中國大陸有什麼影響？俄羅斯未來的經濟結構及其發展方向又是什麼呢？

2012年8月23日，世界貿易組織（WTO）迎來全球最後一位重量級成員——2011年度的全球第九大出口國、19兆美元（約新台幣570兆元）經濟實體的俄羅斯，成為該組織第156位成員。從提出申請到為WTO所接納，中國用了16年，俄羅斯用了18年。俄羅斯並非入世談判最長記錄的保持者，阿爾及利亞的入世之路始於1987年，至今未能如願。

2008年前俄對入世基本上持消極的態度，這主要是俄認為加入世界貿易組織對其經濟沒有太多的好處。在普京執政的八年期間，經濟騰飛基本上是建立在能源和武器產品輸出的基礎之上，俄羅斯的主要交易夥伴為：獨立國協國家、西歐和美國。2011年，中國成為俄羅斯最大的貿易進口國，貿易量超過830億美元。普京對於俄羅斯發展的模式基本上定性為在安全框架之下的穩定經濟增長，現在美國、歐盟陷入經濟危機，此時俄羅斯需要依靠在世貿的框架之下進口設備，給企業未來的發展奠定基礎，這與中國入世擴展海外市場有著巨大的區別。

普京這一發展方向基本結合了來自美國專家、企業寡頭和政府智庫的建議。美國專家給普京的建議是：俄羅斯不需要快速發展GDP，只要政治穩定，經濟不出現意外下降，如發生於1998年的金融危機，那麼在2020年的人均GDP就非常有可能和歐盟持平，此時俄的國力就會自然進入世界前四名內。

企業寡頭則認為，大企業需要將能源、資訊、運輸甚至是農業整合，提高整體效率，希望跨行業經營成為趨勢，這樣企業的利潤在入世貿後也會成倍增長。智庫則更多在國家安全基礎上做文章，指出俄需要在加入世貿之後和現在世界經濟的引擎中國、印度全面合作，但中國和周邊國家複雜的關係成為俄羅斯的主要挑戰；俄羅斯之前有很多的中國通，這些人對於中國文學、文化相當瞭解，但對於中國政治、經濟、人文的瞭解不足，成為中俄發展的主要瓶頸。

2012年7月，兩度被貶職的俄羅斯前財政部長庫德林（Alexei Kudrin），在一次關於俄羅斯就業機會和民族主義問題的新聞發布會上指出，俄羅斯現在加入世界貿易組織是一項政治任務，其實俄羅斯加入世貿談判的進程早就結束了。此前俄羅斯未能加入世貿主要是西方國家的歧視。現在歐盟所經歷的經濟危機一時很難化解，需要向俄市場輸出高科技和基礎設備，來部分化解危機，俄羅斯的能源出口也到了瓶頸，美國、歐盟和俄羅斯基本上也到了相互需要的狀態。此時，俄羅斯需要更主動融入歐洲，融入國際貿易。歐債危機懸而未決，美國經濟增長不穩定，對中國經濟硬著陸的擔憂，給依賴原料出口的俄羅斯帶來不利影響。俄羅斯金融集團銀行總裁涅恰耶夫撰文指出，對於最近幾年始終推行避免風險以及不受歡迎政策的俄羅斯政府來說，全球經濟的不利環境就像是一枚定時炸彈，遲早會被引爆。

現任亞太經合組織工商諮詢委員會主席的馬克門多夫提出，俄羅斯發展主要面臨技術的升級換代和區域發展不平衡的問題。2000年後普京主要解決了蘇聯解體之後的經濟殘局，可以說普京讓俄羅斯經濟止跌回升，但俄羅斯東部、西部發展嚴重失衡和腐敗、官僚問題惡化成為俄羅斯發展的障礙。2008年之後，年輕的梅德維傑夫當選為總統，作為總理的普京曾經希望讓內閣逐漸年輕化和精英化來解決俄羅斯這兩大問題，但似乎成效不大。2012年當普京再次當選為總統之後，希望再次使用國際化手段來達到國家發展的平衡。現在莫斯科的發展基本上資金和技術非常雄厚，如在莫斯科打工的主要以中亞國家和高加索國家的公民為主，這樣當俄羅斯加入世貿後，莫斯科就可以鞏固現有的優勢。俄現在已經鎖定9月8日到9日在遠東舉辦的亞太經合會議作為俄開始和亞洲國家緊密接觸的第一步。

2012年8月10日，俄「報紙網」就發表文章分析「是誰在怕加入世貿」。反對俄羅斯加入世貿的最大力量來自於工會、中小城市政府和中小企業主，他們認為俄羅斯入世之後到2020年俄羅斯進口關稅會降低到2.8%，三年內會有百萬失業人口。

對此，普京和統一黨的看法是，有一些關鍵的談判還需要在加入世貿之後在日內瓦協商，而且國家杜馬（下議院）和聯邦議會（上議院）還需要對很多議項進行表決，政府對於中小企業的保護也持續五年以上，並且2012到2013年俄政府對於中小企業的資助將超過68億歐元。俄羅斯重工業發展所需要的技術，在歐盟國家遇到經濟危機的前提下，俄羅斯可以用大量的現金來購買來自德國、義大利、西班牙國家的技術和設備，政府為掌握重工業企業的寡頭提供了充分的空間，以此來改善自蘇聯解體以來就沒有太大更新的基礎設備。

如果俄希望更有效地利用其地理優勢，那就必須提高對運輸基礎設施的管理，改變鐵路的低效運轉，消除交通的擁堵和海關的貪腐。俄可以將貨物運輸委託由專業化公司操作，在大幅下降的關稅前，貪腐會大大減少，專業化運作會大幅提升俄公司的運作。俄羅斯國內發展所面臨問題主要如下：

首先，國內能源企業如何在賺取大量的現金利潤後轉化為高科技生產的動能。工商諮詢委員會主席馬克門多夫還是「量能集團」的董事會主席，「量能集團」的業務範圍涉及港口、電力、石油開採、建設和資訊業；現在俄羅斯的基礎建設非常符合大企業的發展方向，如果未來俄羅斯和亞洲在運輸、物流和糧食安全進行統一管理，屆時大企業也會獲得空前利益。但是就當前的例子來看，前俄羅斯首富、現在還在監獄之中的尤科斯石油總裁霍多爾科夫斯基在能源企業掘到第一桶金之後，並沒有對企業的研發及設備更新下功夫，反而開始熱衷於2004年的總統選舉。這類富豪空有財富卻未完成產業轉型的例子還有好幾個。

其次，專款不能夠專用。當莫斯科中央政府制定出專項用於技術革新的資金之後，由於某種原因這些資金並不能夠馬上或全部到位，很多地方政府或者是國家企業就把這些不充分的資金用到其他地方。兩度下臺的財長庫德林任上最大的功勞就是用能源企業的盈餘組建了基金，把錢存了起來，為俄財政盈餘做出貢獻。

最後，俄羅斯對於風險投資的資金管理幾乎沒有，這些資金基本上都是由寡頭籌措。俄羅斯的官僚意識制約了創新思想的發展，如果普京能夠在創新思維、風險投資上進行協助，還可以幫助制止腐敗問題的發生。當很多人和筆者討論俄羅斯現在貪污的情況時，有的人說不是很嚴重、有的說非常嚴重。俄羅斯的貪污情況在普京時代和90年代葉利欽時代大為不同，蘇聯解體時，很多人都是利用有限的資本來收購蘇聯遺留下來的資產，此時經常上演小蝦米吃掉大鯨魚的場面；在普京時代，很多的寡頭都是將自己的資產或者國有資產進行組合，然後高價出售，賺取巨額差價，這與90年代把國有資產低價出售時期大大不同。

俄羅斯加入世貿對中國大陸來說，短期之內沒有挑戰，中國大陸的商品依然會大量出口俄羅斯，但長期來講，大陸將會面臨空前的挑戰。2020年後俄羅斯和歐盟將會緊密結合，是朋友也是競爭對手。而中國大陸能夠提供的僅僅是商品，甚至大部分都是低價值、低附加值的商品。俄羅斯作為一個國土面積第一大國，雖然不能夠在近十年之內對於中國製造構成威脅，但其內需市場在俄羅斯加入世貿後對於中國的依賴也將會減少，俄羅斯進口將會更加多元化。俄羅斯現在的發展重點是：設備更新、跨行業發展、深化亞洲國家關係、在國際糾紛中不出頭、以拖待變，對於亞洲國家的糾紛，俄羅斯更多的是扮演旁觀者角色。俄羅斯將未來十年的戰略定位為：發展基礎產業、跨行業經營、不參與國際衝突，等到2020年俄羅斯的人均GDP和歐盟持平後，俄羅斯將全面崛起。

五、俄中關係對台的影響

著有「關於俄台關係和中台關係」一文的俄羅斯東方科學院資深研究員丘多傑耶夫先生認為：中國以和諧社會理論處理國內問題與周邊國家關係，任何威脅和諧理論的分裂（新疆、西藏或是台灣）或是挑釁行為（日本對於釣魚台的國有化問題以及南海島嶼的歸屬問題），中國都採取最強硬的手段來解決，包括軍事打擊。由此觀之，這樣一來是否意味著：中國與周邊國家的關係將會趨於緊張，美國重返亞洲的再平衡政策將會被許多國家用來借題發揮，中國將會更加孤立，任何軍事的衝突都有可能轉化成崩解中國政權的要素。此時俄羅斯對中國的態度就非常關鍵。但是中蘇曾經在珍寶島事件[1]中導致關係的崩解，中國對俄羅斯的關係至今受到嚴重的影響，俄羅斯將會對中國保持謹慎與小心的態度。和諧社會理論包含了威脅中國大陸國家安全的不穩定因素，台灣也是其中之一。

---

[1] 在採訪俄羅斯遠東大學考古與民族學院院長拉林教授的專訪中有段註解：珍寶島位於烏蘇里江，根據中俄之間的條約，兩國之間的邊界是到中國的河岸這邊，所以該島當時應屬於俄羅斯的領土，俄羅斯劃入濱海邊疆區的波扎爾斯基區。1950年代中期以後，中蘇關係惡化，中國升高一連串的內外政策與意識形態的衝突。1969年中蘇邊境在珍寶島發生軍事衝突，3月2日開始蘇聯邊防軍和中國軍隊在島上對峙，戰鬥結果造成雙邊的傷亡，事件到1969年夏末結束，九月雙邊領導人見面，蘇聯政府代表是柯西金 Косыгина А.Н.和中共國務院總理周恩來會晤，商議採取措施解決邊境局勢的正常化。中蘇雙方進行了一連串談判，承認必須要重新審視中蘇邊境問題。談判結果根據烏蘇里江河道與國際法，1991年該島歸屬為中國。

丘多傑耶夫先生在台大石之瑜教授進行的《中國學——口述歷史》計畫中的專訪時說到：

「歷史與兩國雙邊的複雜關係的影響都有作用。很遺憾，社會心理上的理解不若社會政治關係那樣變化快速。鞦韆擺盪的兩國關係持續波動影響至今。在我們的政治環境中，不是學術圈內的意見，表達出中國即將崛起，與中國的關係必須是克制保留和謹慎而為的，做好因應中國領導層換屆的各種關係變化的可能性。在中國政治圈或是不僅在政治圈，與此有關的高層對我們的態度也是不一樣的。比如在中國也有一些出版的地圖冊還是將我國的領土視為中國土地的分支或是影響的範圍。這些地圖仍在出版。關於中蘇之間俄稱達曼斯基的珍寶島軍事衝突（現在算起來應該有四十年了），中方在一些刊物中對中俄戰爭的詮釋很模糊，當然對我們來說，這是很不愉快的陰影。這也不能說——這就是中國現在領導人的意見。應當說，所有的出版物是受到國家控制的。那裡沒有私人出版品，當然這也某種程度在改變。我們不能離開我們的鄰居，中國也是。中國人從二十世紀中總結出重要經驗，這是對於必須要保障國家穩定發展做出的總結。他們已經準備好用一切強硬的手段來避免國家分裂的產生。這個態度表現在新疆和西藏問題上等等。他們想要穩定局勢，包括在中國的周邊穩定——在區域和甚至在較大規模的範圍內。我想，對於雙邊關係未來的持續推展，會是今日我們在雙邊關係中已經觀察到的。」

「中國改革的進行很多是針對今日已經產生的問題而來的，這些問題都呈現在十七大領導的演講和決議中。這些問題讓領導者非常不安。比如，貧富差距的擴大，許多人賺錢非常多，但還有許多人至今仍生活在貧困當中。很多人告訴我至今在黃河流域還生活在黃土洞穴裡，環境條件非常惡劣，這不是今天才有的問題早在七十和八十年代，我和與這些見證的人都見面過。如果要講在今日中國建立新的意識形態，講社會和諧的意識形態特點，它的產生主要也是為了解決今日中國面對的問題，也是因應世界發展的最新形勢。當然在中共領導人的報告中也特別強調了，實現這個理念需要經歷很長的一個時期。假如通過這個理念，首先這是符合社會利益的階段，中國要向前邁進的目標是『偉大的統一』階段，是儒家所講的『大同』世界，或是中共領導人所講的『共產主義』。他們並不排斥使用馬克思列寧的術語強調『共產主義』或是『社會主義』。中華民族的復興也是胡錦濤報告所強調的思想重點。他們不僅在國內推動和諧的理念，也將和諧的概念引入國際關係當中，包括應用在對日本的關係上。

應當說的是，和諧概念的目的是賦予中國領導層要讓自己採取最強硬的手段，來解決所謂破壞他們利益和觸碰這個和諧思想核心的任何問題。這會應用在解決國家領土分裂問題上，包括在新疆和西藏事件上。我們觀察這個強硬的手段與態度，某種程度也存在於對台關係上，中共也會用和諧思想來解決台灣海峽的台灣獨立問題，因為這會損害了中國領導層強調的統一與和諧思想。儘管到目前為止，馬英九也曾提到過，目前仍有不到上千個飛彈瞄準台灣，因此研究與探討這些問題是包含在一個總體的概念當中，這個構想特點不僅反映在中國，同時也反映在中國的周邊環境上。

關於中俄關係，如同我提到的，在俄羅斯有些人擔心中國的崛起會給俄羅斯帶來『國家利己主義』的元素，或是一種『經濟的利己主義』，關於這點我們國家領導者梅德維傑夫總統在2008年六月聖彼得堡舉行的經濟論壇中有說過。不過，也可以從另一方面來看待這個問題。因為高速發展的中國也可以是俄羅斯經濟成長的積極動力！要知道問題的關鍵還是在於，這個例子要如何在我們自己國家的創新發展計畫中落實，我們和中國人一樣，2020年以前要開始完成這些創新建設的戰略目標。難道不值得為此有一個俄羅斯和中國的共同競爭性的『共同發展』模式?!」

「我對於中俄關係向前推進是很樂觀的。但是我也不排除雙邊關係會出現波動，這與中國崛起和我國發展有關。因為我們〔俄羅斯〕目前不可能在創新技術結構方面有很大的發展，來建立技術基礎轉移到競爭性的商品，以此吸引中國人的興趣。我們在這方面潛力落後於中國。我們還停留在原材料，碳氫化合物的供應者狀態。未來的發展？必須說的是，在俄羅斯有些人，並不僅在政治圈內，而且在大眾的意識中，我們可能變成大中國的原料附庸。……在人民群眾裡，特別是在遠東地區，還有這類想法，我們沒什麼人住的土地幾乎有可能會讓中國人占據領土。中國大量移民的可能性有時候嚇壞我們的人民。這些層面存在一席之地。我們多少不喜歡中國方面的行為，我們有時候在報導中會閱讀到。我應該講，這些事件不應該過度放大，我們與中國的關係不是一年，也不是十年。」

「我對中國近十年的變化的評價無疑還是正面的。我為中國和中國人感到高興！我對於我們雙邊關係的發展還是很樂觀的！兩國都需要內部、區域和全球的穩定。最重要的教訓，如同我已經說過了，從二十世紀的百年走來，就是和平和穩定的發展。在未來的十年或許中國可以成長為世界第一大經濟體。他們是否能夠解決今日困擾他們的問題？是否在創新發展中是否做出一個小高峰──那麼，這些問題的回答還是莫衷一是的。至少，西方不會讓他順利成長。今日中國科技還是落後於西方，如同一些研究者的判斷，至少有十五年到二十年的差距。西方將會努力維持這樣的領先差距。作為中俄關係發展的穩定因素是減少區域衝突的發生，台灣應在此做出因應之道，需強化區域整合與減少對立帶來的孤立。」

（本文部分內容刊登於石之瑜教授主持的《中國學──口述歷史》計畫──俄羅斯漢學家的網頁以及中央社《全球中央》雜誌，特此一併感謝台灣大學石之瑜教授、《全球中央》雜誌張淑伶主編與廣州暨南大學吳非教授的指正）

俄羅斯再次崛起？──雙頭鷹的亞太政策與戰略思想

俄羅斯當前在中美關係中的角色

隨著中國的經濟崛起，國際輿論戰結合圍堵政策似乎加速了新型冷戰思維的建構。傳統強權的西方國家並沒有放棄塑造「中國威脅論」[1]對當前世界秩序的危害。美國自九一一事件後身陷中東戰爭的泥淖，維護大型企業與石油利益成為最常詬病小布希政府的因素。復甦美國經濟成為歐巴馬與羅姆尼在總統競選期間最重要爭取選民青睞的辯論核心主軸之

---

[1] 袁鵬指出：「中國威脅論」在美國由來已久，可以追溯到19世紀後期的「排華浪潮」。當時，美國白人種族主義者和勞工利益集團將大批湧向美國西海岸的華工視為對美國主流文化的「威脅」，認為他們是「劣等民族和落後文化的代表」，是白人「飯碗」的搶奪者，於是推動政府分別於1882年和1884年通過了《排華法案》。這一時期的「中國威脅論」是針對華人移民這一特殊族群的，因而不是現代意義上的「中國威脅論」，但其中體現的白人至上主義思想和東西方文明的衝突，則在其後的「中國威脅論」中仍能找到蹤影。

前駐美大使陳錫蕃教授認為，近幾年來西方學界與政界人士對於中國的復興，常以「中國威脅論」稱之。中國威脅論，乃國際關係上一種訴諸對中國採取圍堵的說法，中國大陸因改革開放後經濟崛起，成為國際上具有影響力的大國，同時大量擴充軍備，特別顯示於海空軍在東海及南海的近海聯合防禦作戰能力，使相關國家產生憂慮與質疑，此質疑於1995年因南海問題及對臺灣領海試射飛彈達到高峰。且自2010年起，東南亞多國與中國在南海的爭端升高，更促使這些國家合作對抗軍力不斷增長的中國。日本、南韓已及東盟各國對中共紛紛採取更加防範的態度，並主動向美國尋求保護。美國也順勢加強了與這些亞洲盟友的軍事互動與同盟關係。

蔡正修教授認為，「中國威脅論」是西方國家認為中國崛起將造成威脅的言論的統稱，可以說是一種言論的類型。「中國威脅」（China Threat）的說法雖然在民間流行，但將之做為一種「論述」，則很少見於官方或嚴謹的學術文章當中。探討中國威脅論內涵，可以從對誰的威脅，以及威脅的能力與意圖來看。面對中國大陸實力尤其軍事力量的快速增長，台、美、日直接感受威脅，其他國家感受較少，甚至不認為對其產生威脅，其差異可以有沒有可能的引爆點來解釋。

楊志誠教授認為：根據杭廷頓（Samuel Huntington）的文明衝突，當前三大文明的衝突結構正向不利於美國的基督教文明傾斜，給了中國較寬廣的戰略及戰術空間。就這樣，集結了經濟、政治、文化及軍事的有利因素和情境，中國的國家發展令人感受到有邁向新帝國的景象，這也就是一般所謂的「中國威脅」。

一。美國為了重振全球金融危機後的美國經濟，已經鎖定中國成為美國首要的假想敵人，而製造假想敵是美國與西方國家自冷戰以來對付蘇聯的首項圍堵戰略。近年來，這樣持「中國威脅論」的美國智庫的觀點認為：中國增加軍費造成區域軍事力量的失衡，並以此邏輯推演中國將以武力解決主權爭議和維護現有經濟利益。美國再度以「中國威脅論」作為美國經濟復甦的靶子，自然，中國大陸面臨了國際巨大的壓力。俄羅斯在普京執政後，把遠東作為俄羅斯最重要的戰略要素，俄羅斯的亞太政策更加複雜了亞太區域的局勢，筆者在本文檢視了俄羅斯在中美衝突觀點中的態度與角色。

一、「中國威脅論」在中美衝突概念中的作用

2008年全球金融危機後，中國提出重建經濟秩序的口號，中俄兩國表達了對現存國際世界體系霸權的不滿，並呼籲應當建立新的國際經濟秩序。中俄的合作在國際組織的框架下：包括上海合作組織與金磚國家聯盟機制，中俄的聯合引起美國警惕。隨著普京三度擔任總統職務，西方協助梅德維傑夫連任的輿論策略失敗，儘管如此，美國與俄羅斯維持良好的關係仍是重要的方向，此時，西方所面臨的國際地位與經濟問題將轉向世界工廠的中國，減少對中國經濟的依賴似乎是普遍各國的國際共識。[2]

---

[2] 劍橋大學美國研究計畫部主任Stefan Halper在美國期刊《外交政策》（Foreign Policy）撰文指出：中國戲劇性的崛起使得自身必須使用武力來捍衛既得的利益，中國軍事的威脅已經構成對鄰國的安全問題與區域軍

在美國總統大選之前透露出這樣的訊息，意味著不管是歐巴馬還是羅姆尼當選總統，美國都將對中國採取強硬的外交路線，包括因應可能的軍事衝突。美國似乎對中國的圍堵政策已經形成國際氣候，當中國與周邊國家陸續發生島嶼爭奪權的輿論戰之際，將有可能以武力解決島嶼歸屬問題時，此時美國在亞洲的盟友尋求美國的軍事支持，美國也順理成章以盟友的軍事保護者姿態重返亞洲，在日本擅自將釣魚臺國有化的獨斷行徑下，刺激了中國民族主義和鷹派份子，那麼此時的圍堵是否會演變成中美直接的軍事衝突？俄羅斯目前在中美衝突中的態度與角色同樣值得關注。

事的失衡，而中國的經濟崛起對許多落後與發展中國家象徵著集權統治帶來經濟成長的典範，這對西方世界的民主價值觀已經造成威脅，他強調中國對於美國應該不是夥伴，而是對手和敵人。

這樣的「中國威脅論」無獨有偶，美國亞洲研究局（NBR-The National Bureau of Asian Research）則出版了《China's Military Challenge》，該書提到中國解放軍的實力改變了美國在亞太軍事均衡的力量與現存的世界秩序，美國對中國過度的經濟依賴使得美國赤字問題仍然無法得到有效解決，美國的「亞洲再平衡」政策是維護美國利益的關鍵。顯然，美國決策層正在形成打擊中國的輿論，並將此視為恢復美國利益的推動力量。儘管美國學者Joseph S. Nye在《The Future of Power》一書中強調，中國的實力仍然落後美國幾十年，中國仍然面對內部許多的問題需要解決，過度吹噓中國的威脅將鼓勵兩國鷹派的抬頭，不利於區域安全與和平穩定。

美國華府重要智庫如Woodrow Wilson Center的亞洲計畫再度將視角放在中國軍事現代化對美國與亞太地區的衝擊上，根據智庫中國研究者的態度與反應顯示，目前美國已經將中國鎖定為亞太地區主要的軍事威脅者，為此華府似乎正在形成關於「中國威脅論」的基本論述來宣傳這樣的概念，美國方面甚至派人到俄羅斯進行相關的遊說。

Randall L. Schweller認為，臺灣和日本不能排除與中國開戰的可能，此時美國被捲入戰火的機會就很大。另外，學者也指出，由於權力擴張的天性與國家成長的需要，興起中的強權本身便構成國際體系中的不穩因素，中國大陸的快速崛起將對國際體系原有的霸權國家美國造成挑戰。

俄羅斯再次崛起？──雙頭鷹的亞太政策與戰略思想

儘管中俄之間仍存在歧見與問題，中俄關係仍有發展和改善的空間，普京重返克林姆林宮之後，強調以外交政治談判取代戰爭的國際行動將成為外交主軸，與亞太地區的經貿關係利益將大於區域爭霸的動機，普京的亞洲政策將成為俄羅斯實現全球治理戰略的重要因素，尤其在2008年全球金融危機之後，中俄之間都看到了重建國際經濟秩序的機會，然而俄羅斯和中國在內部都面對著反對派的抗議聲浪，西方介入反對派的威脅也成為兩國領導人未來的執政壓力，而俄羅斯與中國之間在國際領域的合作將是穩定各自內部發展的最為關鍵的因素。預期中俄未來在聯合國安全理事會的合作力度將大大的增加，而區域之間的合作機制如上海合作組織以及金磚國家聯盟的發展將會獲得重視，成為中俄增加互動與加強聯繫的重要平台與聯繫機制。

　　「中國威脅論」是否會成為美國選後的方針，目前看來，至少中國要在經濟利益方面做出某些退讓。俄羅斯又如何看待中美關係的對峙也是令人關注。在普京執政的八年期間，經濟騰飛基本上是建立在能源和武器產品輸出的基礎之上，俄羅斯的主要交易夥伴為：獨聯體國家、西歐和美國。普京對於俄羅斯發展的模式基本上定性為在安全框架之下的穩定經濟增長，現在美國、歐盟陷入經濟危機，此時俄羅斯需要依靠在世貿的框架之下進口設備，給企業未來的發展奠定基礎，這與中國入世擴展海外市場有著巨大的區別。

二、俄羅斯在亞太政策的變化與影響

　　Lipman & Petrov（2011）認為，俄羅斯當局對於中國在亞太戰略中的策略將有所轉變，主要是莫斯科方面認為中國形成了改變鄧小平「韜光養晦」外交策略，這將使得亞洲國家普遍感到威脅而尋求美國的支持，俄羅斯並不想與美國衝突，莫斯科方面將以加強印度、越南、東盟和韓國的關係來平衡亞洲的局勢，由於梅德維傑夫總統任內過於親近西方國家而被視為「另一個戈巴契夫」，梅德維傑夫以登上千島群島也就是日稱的北方四島，顯示自己處理爭議領土的強勢能力，此舉曾被視為梅德維傑夫希望連任的象徵。儘管如此，普京重回總統寶座也不會過度與美國正面衝突。日俄之間的島嶼矛盾問題使得俄羅斯將首先發展韓國關係，這樣一來，俄羅斯將在南北韓問題上偏向韓國，朝鮮為發展經濟必定與俄羅斯和美國有所退讓，韓國將成為美俄兩國協調亞洲問題的重要盟友。許多學者認為，俄羅斯不會完全隨著美國策略行走，此時中俄在經濟關係上強化了合作力度，對美國無疑是一種抵抗。[3]

---

[3] 高麗大學名譽教授，前外務部長官韓升洲在《朝鮮日報》撰文表示，韓國要在北核問題、北韓改革開放、遏制北韓挑釁等問題上，引導俄羅斯發揮更積極的作用。

　　Marcel de Haas指出，「中國威脅論」在普京執政後主要發酵在遠東地區非法移民問題上。俄羅斯輿論擔憂遠東人口太少，如果不正視非法移民的問題，遠東將被中國人逐漸和平佔領。2005年12月，俄羅斯內政部長努爾加里耶夫表示遠東移民構成了俄羅斯遠東安全的威脅。

　　Stephen Blank在美國軍事戰爭學院與戰略研究院（U.S. Army War College and Strategy Studies Institute）的研究報告指出，俄羅斯對中國以及亞洲國家的武器銷售全然沒有考慮中國與俄羅斯的歷史上累積的敵普京執政之後，開始採取雙頭鷹政策，與亞洲國家領導者有實際的交往和政策，對中俄關係發展問題的重視顯示在：如何再提高中俄貿易額度的同時，兼具考慮到俄羅斯自身的國家安全與地緣戰略運用的意涵。俄羅斯《全球事務雜誌》（Russia in Global Affairs）主編Fyodor Lukyanov撰文指出，認為俄羅斯應該擺脫以中國為中心的亞洲政策，否則只能在經濟上成為中國的小兄弟。普京上任初期，也將俄羅斯的亞太安全戰略定位在提升遠東地區的作用。儘管亞洲戰略目標長久以來聲明大於行動，但這樣的觀點似乎在俄入世之後趨於明顯，並在今年九月符拉迪沃斯托克／海參崴舉行的亞太經合會議之後逐漸落實。俄羅斯在全球金融危機後將經濟目標轉向亞洲，目前俄羅斯外交部呼籲中國和日本要冷靜和平處理釣魚臺問題，俄羅斯有評論認為，亞洲目前是世界經濟的主要動力，中日若爆發戰爭將引起新的全球經濟危機，中俄將在這場危機中遭受巨大損害。

　　衛斯里大學教授Peter Rutland認為，俄羅斯融入亞洲成為提升俄羅斯全球競爭力的關鍵因素，從領土來看俄羅斯領土有

對關係，也沒有考慮到這些亞洲國家與中國的緊張關係，顯示俄羅斯缺乏戰略眼光和政府決策的無能，這都是蘇聯解體後俄羅斯政府結構失衡和貪污腐敗的結果，反映出俄羅斯亞洲政策是失敗的。這種觀點建立在俄羅斯經濟對中國的依賴和缺乏長遠安全戰略基礎上來看。

　　Richard Weitz認為，俄羅斯對中國的軍售是否影響東亞軍事平衡也是美國關注的問題，對俄羅斯而言，中國是最重要的武器出口市場，就上海合作組織的基礎而言，中俄關係的友好有助於雙方的軍事互信與武器銷售。

　　Zevelev & Troitskiy認為，2000年普京執政後，俄羅斯普遍社會心理發生了轉變，認為俄羅斯依靠能源政策將可以有自己的獨立外交，不必再服務於其他強權國家，也沒有任何其他國家可以逼迫俄羅斯做自己不想做得事，這樣轉變影響了俄羅斯對美國的政策，也包括面對核武不擴散條約以及處理中亞和中東問題上的強硬態度。

五分之一在亞洲板塊上，人口僅有八百萬人，俄羅斯在西伯利亞石油出口亞洲將繼續帶動俄羅斯的經濟成長。美國不應該將俄羅斯推向中國，對俄羅斯的緩和政策將支撐美國對中國圍堵政策的基礎。目前美國對俄羅斯應不會採取新的圍堵政策，不論在華府智庫所散發出的訊息，或是在美方重要人士到莫斯科試圖尋求合作的舉措來看，都顯示美國目前並不準備執行對俄羅斯新的圍堵政策，反倒是希望與俄羅斯未來在經貿關係方面加強合作。按此方向發展，美國傾向美俄共同合作來圍堵中國，然而，俄羅斯是否有必要參與美國圍堵中國的政策？這對俄羅斯是否有好處？

顯然，俄羅斯在中美衝突中扮演非常關鍵的角色，沒有俄羅斯的支持，中國似乎更加孤立於國際環境的敵對氣氛中。中國方面有評論者認為，中美之間的軍事衝突將面臨重蹈晚清八國聯軍的覆轍。中國是否會因此在被列強瓜分利益之後導致俄羅斯在這場軍事衝突當中而盡占漁翁之利：俄羅斯因調停而鯨吞蠶食和坐享其成？「中國威脅論」與「黃禍論」在俄羅斯一向存在基本的民意，主要由於遠東地區的經濟對於中國的依賴，它的作用在於當中國對於中俄領土問題採取民族主義策略時，俄羅斯中央就會採取對中國相應的極端政策。中俄有可能因此陷入軍事衝突與中俄冷戰，中俄關係惡化的結果反而有利於中美關係的緩和，這是俄羅斯最不願看到結果。

俄羅斯有評論指出俄羅斯不應該成為中美衝突的炮灰，否則俄羅斯會在中美衝突的處境中成為爭奪的戰場，對此俄羅斯應該考慮自己的利益，不要成為中國和美國任何一方的犧牲品。過去兩極冷戰時期，美蘇是冷戰敵對關係，蘇聯解體之後，美國繼續帶領北約組織東擴，甚至在小布希執政期間擅自退出反導條約，在東歐國家佈署飛彈。是故美國從來沒有放棄圍堵俄羅斯的策略，俄羅斯已經為此付出巨大的代價。在蘇聯解體後，俄羅斯將自己的戰略範圍縮小在前蘇聯的加盟共和國當中，普京為了維護俄羅斯既有的利益與國家發展上升的態勢，還必須犧牲民主體制回鍋擔任第三任總統，使俄羅斯仍然走向蘇聯時期中央集權的老路，對於俄羅斯未來民主體制與接班人的養成機制蒙上陰影，使俄羅斯的政治在將來普京之後仍然走向不確定性，不利於俄國長遠的政權穩定與民主發展。但普京的思路應該是：當代俄羅斯內部經濟發展到一定高度時，並且完成現代化的工程建設，政府機制運轉成熟，下位接班人可以穩定國家的治理。

歷史殷鑒不遠，俄羅斯正謹慎評估中美摩擦並且要為美國經濟復甦做好準備，美國對於俄羅斯民主派和右翼支持隨時會成為普京三度執政後的潛在威脅，美國隨時可以採取顏色革命的方式來影響俄羅斯政治的走向以及新政權的產生，這是俄羅斯最為擔憂的和平政變，如果俄羅斯在中美衝突中過於親近美國，俄羅斯又將成為下個美國圍堵的對象，到時候俄羅斯將會非常的被動。俄羅斯媒體有評論認為，美國共和黨向來對俄羅斯採取敵對政策，如果羅姆尼當選總統之後，俄美關係將會更為複雜。不過，普京已經先行當選總統了，不論誰當選美國總統，普京總統將會採取務實的對美關係政策。如果美國將對中國採取更為強硬的政策，俄羅斯將不會強出頭與美國碰撞，同樣希望拉攏美俄關係緩和的步伐勢必緩慢，這將減輕中國因應來自美國與其他週邊國家的挑釁。

普京上任初期，基於中俄關係的不確定性，改變了葉利欽與江澤民關於中俄石油管道的協議，認為從安加爾斯克通往太平洋港口的納霍德卡的石油出口管道才是最符合俄羅斯地緣政治的利益，從這裏再出口石油到日本、美國以及其他亞太地區國家，再從斯科沃羅季諾鋪設一條距離中國邊境七十公里的支線管道到大慶。俄羅斯對於東西伯利亞到太平洋的石油管道鋪設戰略概念基本是在發展遠東經濟的主導權與石化加工製造產業以及對中國政治的不確認和不信任的基礎上建構的。從未來俄羅斯石油將成為中國主要的出口國的長遠利益而言，俄羅斯認為在中美衝突中採取親美態度將不利於自身未來的戰略安全。但俄羅斯的在中美衝突中的不支持態度對中國也構成壓力。俄羅斯對貝加爾湖到遠東蘇維埃港的鐵路建設，也有利於薩哈林島油田的開發，對於打通莫斯科到遠東的道路而言，提高了整體國家的安全戰略和控制。

　　目前中國對此投資意願不高是基於自身戰略佈局。俄羅斯則希望藉此吸引亞洲的合作。

三、中國面臨美俄的挑戰仍大

　　美國總統大選後，美國將面臨東北亞、南北韓問題、釣魚島問題以及南海諸島所屬問題的衝擊。美國目前將外交陣線由歐巴馬第一任的阿富巴戰略轉移到亞太地區，中亞遺留下來的恐怖主義問題將順勢交給中俄共同主導的上海合作組織來面對。普京強勢執政之後，俄羅斯更加強化遠東地區的地緣戰略優勢來提升俄羅斯的亞太影響力，中美之間的新型冷戰關係將對臺灣產生直接的衝擊與影響。白宮安全顧問Victor Cha對筆者表示，美國不方便過多的干涉，希望中日韓有合作的新架構。由此觀之，美國並不希望進入全面的戰爭狀態，否則會引起二戰之後韓戰促使亞洲冷戰陣線全面的開啟，美國將耗費更大的成本來進行亞洲軍事的對抗，這對於美國金融危機之後所面臨的國內經濟問題轉型是非常不利的。

美國對於亞太地區佈局的考慮應該不僅是軍售的利益，而是整體美國在亞洲所具有的信用為美國帶來整體的國家利益，美國將在總統大選後減少對中國經濟的依賴。顯然，美國對中國的強硬態度顯示，美國正在為亞太經濟關係重組以及吸引美國資金回流本土投資做好準備，這意味著美國將在總統大選之後從2008年以來金融危機的經濟低谷走向經濟的全面復甦，美國減少對中國的經濟依賴成為下屆總統任內的必然趨勢。亞洲國家正在為美國經濟復甦後取代中國的經濟空間向美國頻頻招手示好。

筆者在美觀看總統兩次辯論節目時發現，中國是羅姆尼提到次數最多的國家，顯然中國問題成為美國復甦的首要對抗目標，那麼，美國對於大陸的軍事圍堵事實上也是為吸引美國國內資金回流、改善中小企業的生存環境以及提高基層就業率做出的一種策略，這樣一來，就可以理解為何共和黨總統候選人羅姆尼要在總統大選的競選策略中採取減稅的口號，起初這樣的減稅口令中產階層非常懷疑是偏向美國大企業的騙術，畢竟小布希總統的反恐戰爭與爆發的金融危機還令美國中產非常反感，後來經過十月進行的兩場總統電視辯論會之後，羅姆尼的政策逐漸發酵，顯示主軸在於減少對中國的投資而轉向美國本土。同樣地，歐巴馬的福利政策一直對美國基層具有吸引力，後來經過辯論之後，輿論突然戲劇性的演變成為導致中產階層負擔過重的原因。不論是歐巴馬或是羅姆尼，都試圖在總統競選過程中，讓搖擺的選民支持自己，雙方都積極證明自己最有能力解決基層就業問題並且裨益中產階層。如何使中國在經濟上對美作出讓步，外部的危機將使中美衝突更加明顯。

由於中國已經成為世界最大的製造工廠，如何把美國在中國經濟利益重新轉向到美國本土，成為美國經濟復甦的關鍵動力。美國對於中國的圍堵以及亞太島嶼之爭的白熱化似乎都有美國重返亞洲與振興經濟的因素在內。美國對於日本的底線是否引起中國軍事對抗，以及是否這種對抗會再度引起冷戰，在中國尚未全面擴大內需之下，中國大陸應如何面對未來因為島嶼爭議問題而引發的經濟危機，這成為了中國新任領導者的挑戰。中國目前已經展開與俄羅斯的溝通，並加強與俄羅斯有更多緊密的持續溝通，以期在美國圍堵政策中找到突圍出口。

四、上海合作組織的影響與方向

近年來，上海合作組織的職能已經逐步的擴大與形成影響力，筆者認為研究上合組織的方向也逐漸從中亞與中俄為核心逐漸轉向俄羅斯對於中亞與中國的影響為研究核心，主要原因與俄羅斯歐亞戰略與亞洲新戰略構成了俄羅斯的全球戰略的核心，隨著俄羅斯的崛起與普京強人政治的再次復甦而得到強

俄羅斯再次崛起？——雙頭鷹的亞太政策與戰略思想

化。許多研究者都發現，中亞國家對於提升能源戰略的首要因素是俄羅斯的態度，顯示俄羅斯在上合組織中的地位會逐步強化。[4]

　　中亞過去的發展主要分為兩個階段：第一個階段是蘇聯解體之後與俄羅斯經濟空間整合的一體化過程，主要目的在於解決盧布流通使用與降低邊境貿易關稅與通過等問題，其次是俄羅斯對於中亞國家軍隊培訓的問題；第二個階段是美國在九一一事件之後介入中亞，除了仰賴中亞的軍事基地與共同演習合作以外，最重要的目的在於以經濟援助推進中亞地區的民

---

[4] 傅仁坤所長在「中亞五國對上合組織之立場」以及與張益銘合寫的〈中亞區域安全與上海合作組織的發展〉，強調上合組織未來必定逐漸增強國際影響力，儘管成員國當中存在政經體制與宗教文化以及經濟利益的差異。

　　趙志凌副教授「上合組織的能源議題」切入中亞與上合組織，引述中國經濟報導的觀點認為「未來發展趨勢可能會依照俄羅斯總統普京在2006年的上海峰會時倡議，在上合組織框架內創建能源俱樂部，主要目標在於協調組織成員國的行為，達成能源市場的穩定。」

　　Erkin Ekrem，則是來自於土耳其，他寫了一篇關於「土耳其與伊朗對上海合作組織的政策立場」的文章，作者從地緣政治與能源利益的基礎上研究分析了中美俄的大國角力以及土耳其在歷史民族文化傳統的意義上所持的態度。

　　張雅君所長在「上海合作組織實踐的困境與前景」一文中認為，上合組織在九一一事件之後無法發揮效果，美國對於中亞在當時的影響力卻逐漸增加，中國確無力影響，長期而言，上合組織對於中亞國家確是有意的。

　　傅馨儀副研究員從中亞的角度出發，寫了「上合組織經貿關係」一文，研究了上合組織對於俄羅斯強化中亞經貿關係產生的作用：包括石油管道鋪設、完善法律機制、加大投資力度、調整產業結構與資源合理配置、以及改善投資環境和交通道路等等。

　　連弘儀助理教授則進一步強調了共同反恐機制走向國際合作中的經濟合作與國際議題的共識，他在「俄中在上海合作組織反恐機制下合作之研究」一文中以反恐作為中俄聯合軍演的核心基礎論述該組織的特點與方向。

　　汪毓瑋教授撰寫的「美國對上合組織的政策立場」，強調了美國中亞戰略的設計從共同反恐到對中亞國內民主問題的介入，深刻地反映了美國對於中亞的影響。

主化進程，顏色革命方式的政權轉移成為投資重要方向，這已經被俄羅斯在國際能源價格上漲產生的經濟實力以及俄羅斯現代化軍隊改革對於中亞的控制所瓦解，美國在歐巴馬政權之後逐漸在金融風暴與俄喬戰爭的衝擊下退出中亞地區。中亞的阿富汗和伊朗核安全將逐漸仰賴俄羅斯與上合組織的合作，中亞再度回到俄羅斯勢力範圍，因此研究俄羅斯與莫斯科當局的政策，又回到研究的核心，過去利用中亞與中國對於俄羅斯的矛盾方向已經必須要轉向到俄羅斯執政核心對於上合組織的影響與普京的亞洲新戰略方向上。中美俄的競合從中亞拉到了東亞，此時，中國的崛起與美國的重返亞洲導致中美衝突的加劇，中俄防止美國會佈置導彈防禦系統。

政大的獨立國協研究中心主任王定士教授對筆者表示，目前俄羅斯希望在聯合國架構下解決國際爭端的意圖與動作越來越成形，中國在聯合國中的角色也特別關鍵。俄羅斯外長拉夫羅夫2010年9月21日在聯合國千年發展目標峰會上表示，全球發展與安全問題息息相關，經濟問題所引發社會問題包括疾病、低收入戶的增加、失控移民和恐怖主義蔓延都會導致全球經濟危機。經濟危機成為安全危機的關鍵因素。

上海合作組織的趨勢大抵可以反映如下：

第一、上合組織逐漸對於東北亞局勢產生的影響，中美若是冷戰，關鍵在於俄羅斯的態度；

第二、中美關係若是趨於惡化，目前中俄一期油管已經建成，俄羅斯是否會減少對中國軍售與石油輸出，在影響俄羅斯的利益之下，俄羅斯會轉向與兩韓以及東南亞國家的合作，以彌補在中美冷戰中的損失；

第三、中美俄競合的地點若在東北亞展開，東北亞有朝核危機與日俄韓有北方四島與釣魚台等諸多的島嶼領土爭議，中俄對於朝核問題有絕對的影響力，日本受到中俄排擠勢必求助於美國，日韓之間儘管有獨島爭議，美國的介入就更加關鍵了。美國介入必須避開俄羅斯，美俄關係若趨緩和，中美關係若趨於緊張，中國勢必尋求俄羅斯的支持。

第四、南海問題凸顯了中國的外交危機，美國積極介入斡旋，加速了中美之間的衝突，中共當局勢必轉向俄羅斯，這樣一來，中美俄的國際競合重點又再度回到亞太地區了。

　　這樣的假設的產生主要來自於兩個重要事件：第一是普京回鍋擔任總統與出訪中國大陸進行國是訪問並且出席了上合組織第十二屆領袖高峰會；俄羅斯正式成為第156個WTO會員國。首先，普京的長期執政帶來了許多影響，包括國際體系逐漸由冷戰體系後的單極化走向多極化，俄羅斯的意見和影響在國際社會中越來越重要，這對於中國與美國以及乃至於亞太地區的影響是什麼？

　　其次，台灣的貿易競爭力逐年下滑，俄羅斯絕對是亞洲通往歐洲最近的渠道。台灣應思考俄羅斯在提升台灣地緣戰略上的經濟作用和外交作用。冷戰體系與新冷戰體系當中美俄仍是競爭對象，本文目的是要探討俄羅斯的亞洲戰略對於亞太地區以及包括台灣的影響又是什麼？全球金融危機與俄喬戰爭之後，俄羅斯的崛起已經形成美國外交政策的轉向，美國戰略逐漸轉向對中國大陸施壓。目前俄羅斯與哈薩克斯坦在上合組織的機制內達成能源俱樂部的戰略目標，中哈兩國已探明石油位居世界前三位，俄羅斯石油出口則是全球第一位，俄羅斯天然氣儲量與出口佔據世界第一位，中國是世界最大的能源進口國，無庸置疑，在上合組織架構下，在2012年中俄之間已經初步完成輸出與輸入的互動機制，中俄對於國際能源的價格與世界政治經濟格局的影響無疑地已經非常巨大了。

五、俄羅斯在亞太作用將增強

　　俄羅斯前駐平壤與首爾經濟代表Toloraya[5]則認為，金大中的陽光政策使得俄羅斯成為平衡東北亞勢力的重要夥伴，成為解決朝核危機的關鍵角色，1998-2003年是俄羅斯進入東北亞的關鍵時期。俄羅斯學者Luzyanin認為，普京2000年上任後，外交政策最大的改變就是轉向東方。Sevastyanov認為，普京2001年出席上海舉行的APEC會議簽署了一系列經濟協議，把提升遠東經濟現代化目標納入政策領域當中，旨在加強與亞太地區國家之間合作，為此俄羅斯必須改善西伯利亞通往亞洲的鐵路運輸道路。Voronin認為，俄羅斯與東盟成為對話夥伴關係是建立新型關係的體現。

---

[5] Toloraya接受筆者邀請訪台時曾告訴筆者，俄羅斯的亞太政策不會與中國爭取經濟地位，但會扮演平衡區域經濟利益的協調角色。台俄經貿合作關鍵在於台灣方面。

2005年，普京出席了俄羅斯與東盟國家領袖高峰會，強調俄羅斯會加強與東南亞國家之間在區域和平、穩定與安全方面的合作，俄羅斯為此通過了《俄羅斯與東盟2005-2015戰略合作發展計畫》，旨在落實反恐、經貿、能源、投資等領域的互動與合作關係。Osintseva認為，普京執政最大政策的改變就是深入亞太地區以提升俄羅斯遠東地區的經濟發展與戰略價值。總體觀之，美國在911事件之後，俄羅斯與中國都在此間快速發展與崛起，俄羅斯的亞太政策與美國的亞洲再平衡政策增加了美國下屆總統的挑戰，中美俄在亞太地區的角力也顯示了亞洲未在來經濟與政治上的重要性和複雜性。

　　隨著中國的經濟崛起，給中國帶來的挑戰與機會是雙重的。中美俄都將在新的執政期間壯大國家發展。美國新一輪「中國威脅論」主要根據國際局勢變化下自身重返亞洲「再平衡」的外交政策與美國本土經濟復甦的需求而來的，俄羅斯也會根據中美關係來謹慎評估與中國的戰略關係。俄羅斯不會在美國與中國之間瀕欲升高的軍事衝突中與美國過於親近，但是俄羅斯為獲取更多亞洲市場的利益，會加強與印度、越南、東盟以及韓國的關係，由於在日俄島嶼爭議的矛盾情緒之下，俄羅斯尤其會以發展韓國關係最為首要，朝鮮也會為了減少對中國的經濟依賴逐漸強化與美國和俄羅斯的關係。

　　金日恩政權的導彈和核武也是要減少依賴中國而迫使西方經援的一種手段。俄羅斯仍會觀望中國是否在改變「韜光養晦」的外交政策下發展軍事，會以此作為指標來減少對中國出售先進武器和提高石油價格，以此牽制中國和避免激怒美國和亞太國家。畢竟中國從長遠來看仍是俄羅斯最大的石油與武器銷售市場，此時，中國面對俄羅斯入世後的產業多元化以及美國逐漸將資金吸引回本土的經濟政策，中國必須持續加強與俄羅斯進行更多緊密的交流溝通與經貿合作，來確保中國發展內需經濟的戰略所需要的穩定外部環境，上海合作組織仍是平衡美國單邊政策最為重要的區域國際合作機制，以期中俄之間的加強溝通與合作應是中國目前最需要的外交任務，以此觀之，中國將更重視與俄羅斯的關係，以此因應美國對中國的外部圍堵所可能產生的中國內部混亂和經濟下滑的危機爆發。

參考文獻

1. 陳錫蕃、謝志傳，〈中國威脅論面面觀〉，國家政策研究基金會，August 31, 2012。

2. 韓升洲，〈普亭外交政策重心重返亞洲〉，韓國《朝鮮日報》中文網路版，03/16/2012。

3. 蔡政修，〈中國威脅論的省思〉。

4. 楊志誠，〈論中國崛起與中國威脅〉，《海峽評論》184期，2006年4月號。

5. 袁鵬，〈中國威脅論的歷史演變〉，《環球時報》，2002年08月01日。

6. 傅仁坤，〈中亞五國對上合組織之立場〉。

7. 趙志凌，〈上合組織的能源議題〉。

8. Erkin Ekrem，〈土耳其與伊朗對上海合作組織的政策立場〉。

9. 張雅君，〈上海合作組織實踐的困境與前景〉。

10. 傅馨儀，〈上合組織經貿議題〉。

11. 連弘儀，〈俄中在上海合作組織反恐機制下合作之研究〉。

12. 汪毓瑋，〈美國對上合組織的政策立場〉。

13. 胡逢瑛，〈大國再起？蒲亭訪中意在全球〉，（中央社《全球中央》雜誌2012年8月號）。

14. 胡逢瑛、吳非，〈俄羅斯入世之路：耗時18年，著眼後20年〉，（中央社《全球中央》雜誌2012年9月號）。

15. Ashley Tellis & Travis Tanner (2012). *China's Military Challenge*, NBR-The National Bureau of Asian Research, (pp.1-22). Washington D.C.

16. Lipman & Petrov (2011). *Russia in 2020*, (pp.51-52). Washington D.C., Carnegie Endowment for International Peace.

17. Taiwan's Approach to Escalating Sovereignty Disputes in East Asia, Event in CSIS, (10/17/2012). Washington D.C.

18. Stefan Halper(2011). "The China Threat", Foreign Policy, (MARCH/APRIL 2011).

    http://www.foreignpolicy.com/articles/2011/02/22/the_china_threat

19. Fyodor Lukyanov, "Uncertain World: The disputed Kuril Islands and Russia's broader Asian strategy", 《Russia in Global Affairs》, (Moscow, 11/11/2010).

    http://en.rian.ru/columnists/20101111/161292198.html

20. Sergei Karaganov, "Russia's Asian Strategy", *Russia in Global Affairs*, (07/02/2010).

    http://eng.globalaffairs.ru/pubcol/Russias-Asian-Strategy-15254

21. Stephen Blank, "Why Russia's Policy is Falling in China", (04/02/1997).

    http://www.strategicstudiesinstitute.army.mil/pdffiles/00146.pdf

22. Peter Rutland, "Russia's Economic Role in Asia: Toward Deeper Integration", NBR-Strategy Asia 2006-2007.

    http://prutland.web.wesleyan.edu/Documents/NBRfinal.pdf

23. Marcel de Haas, "Russia-China Security Cooperation", Power and Interest News Report, (November 27, 2006).

    www.pinr.com/report.php?ac=view_report&report_id=588&language_id=1.

24. Richard Weitz, China-Russia Security Relations: Strategy Parallelism Without Partnership or Passion?
   http://www.strategicstudiesinstitute.army.mil/pdffiles/pub868.pdf

25. Randall L. Schweller(1999). "Managing the Rise of Great Power: History and Theory," Engaging China:The Management of an Emerging Power. Eds. Alastair Iain Johnston and Robert S. Ross. Routledge:London and New York.

26. Toloraya, "Collection of Essays on Russian Policy in Korea: 1998-2003".
   http://world.lib.ru/k/kim_o_i/a972.shtml

27. Админ(2012). "Президент Путин: взгляд из США". Источник: www.svobodanews.ru
   http://40-region.ru/news/v_mire/30437-prezident-putin-vzglyad-iz-ssha.html

28. Воронин А.С. (2010) АСЕАН в начале XXI века. Актуальные проблемы и перспективы., (с. 288-308). Москва.

29. Зевелёв &Троицкий(Москва, 2006)., "СИЛА И ВЛИЯНИЕ В АМЕРИКАНО-РОССИЙСКИХ ОТНОШЕНИЯ",
   http://www.obraforum.ru/pdf/Semiotics-US-Russian-relations-WP2.pdf

30. Комплексная программа действий по развитию сотрудничества Российской Федерации и Ассоциации государств Юго-Восточной Азии на 2005-2015 гг. : полный текст. [Электронный ресурс]. URL:

http://www.indonesia.mid.ru/russia-asean/ docs-05.html (дата обращения: 19.12.2011).

31. Лузянин С.Г.(2007). Восточная политика В.В. Путина. Возвращение России на «Большой Восток» (2004-2008), (с. 365). Москва.

32. Севастьянов С.В.(2003). Международно-политические аспекты перспективного развития Дальнего Востока, (с. 29-40). Хабаровск.

Совместная декларация главы государства Российской Федерации и глав государств и правительств государств-членов Ассоциации государств Юго-Восточной Азии о развитом и всеобъемлющем партнерстве от 13 декабря 2005 г. : полный текст. [Электронный ресурс]. URL: http://www.indonesia.mid.ru/russia-asean/docs-04.html (дата обращения: 18.12.2011).

33. Осинцева Н. С. "ПОЛИТИКА РОССИИ В ЮГО-ВОСТОЧНОЙ АЗИИ В НАЧАЛЕ XXI В." http://www.teoria-practica.ru/-8-2012/politics/osintseva.pdf

34. Толорая Г. Д. (2011). "Россия и БРИКС: стратегия взаимодействия" ，Журнал Стратегия России, №8, Август.

俄羅斯建構金磚國家聯盟之意涵

蘇聯解體之後，短短二十年之內俄羅斯又重新與美國競逐佔領世界領導的位置。2008年，美國金融危機與俄喬戰爭的爆發可以作為這樣新國際秩序的分水嶺。俄羅斯內部經過二十年的內部調整與能量積蓄，努力堅毅謀求蓄勢待發的過程是俄羅斯恢復強大的總體特點，也是俄羅斯國家發展的長期戰略特點。俄羅斯轉型特點在三任國家領導者執政方針與戰略思維當中反映出來。葉利欽總統在執政十年間進行全面政治經濟改革的轉軌工作，普京在八年總統與四年總理任內則全面執行能源外交政策與恢復國家化政策，商業化成為國家化政策的輔助，國家利益大於企業寡頭利益的概念成為普京強國政策特點；國家安全則是政府控制內部腐化與外部攻擊的核心機制；鞏固前蘇聯的版圖勢力範圍在獨聯體的軍事和經濟一體化政策獲得落實。

梅德韋傑夫擔任總統期間則貫徹現代化與創新重組的概念，把俄羅斯全面推進了全球化進程當中，以現代化國家與全球合作取代對抗的正面形象作為國家發展的長期方向，為俄羅斯下個十年發展奠定了全球發展戰略的基礎。俄羅斯以金磚國家作為經濟合作基礎，企圖重建國際新經濟秩序，爭取更有利的國際條件，以期擺脫依賴能源作為經濟基礎的短期策略。俄羅斯在近十年內成為影響國際格局的大國，僅管能源政策發揮了關鍵作用，但未來俄羅斯將全面落實全球化政策與加強全球佈局能力，俄羅斯的國際化道路與全球合作勢在必行，故以能源與武器作為與俄羅斯合作的前提目標將會受挫，這裡面有國家安全與國家戰略意義的衝突，故須以國際化和全球化觀點與俄羅斯進行全方面合作才有收穫，不論科技技術、人文藝術或是教育研究，都可以遍地開花，吾人也將在全球化的相互交流合作進程中成為參與者和受益者。

俄羅斯則將在文化和傳統中找到自信，金磚國家聯盟的概念將成為俄羅斯發揮外交傳統和經驗的表演舞台；俄羅斯文化和文明的優勢會幫助俄羅斯人重拾信心，金磚國家在文化古國的概念下發展成區域重要的一極，以平衡美國的單極世界。2012年3月4日，普京在總統大選中獲得壓倒性的勝利，重返克里姆林宮之後，強化發展亞洲戰略以及提高俄羅斯與亞洲國家合作成為重點，能源政策是導引基礎，俄羅斯將強化在亞洲的影響力並且與美國分庭抗禮則是未來國際格局的新趨勢。中國政府已經選擇向俄羅斯靠攏以謀求軍方對中央新領導階層的支持。台灣在這股新趨勢下應可加強與俄羅斯的合作與聯繫，以期在美俄競逐與中美貿易衝突的國際架構下平衡兩岸關係與穩定國家發展。

一、金磚國家的國際影響力

金磚四國的概念在兩千年被美國高盛公司提出之後，引起全球投資與各國競相交往的目標。2008年，在美國爆發了全球性金融危機後，俄羅斯和中國看到了建構國際新經濟秩序的機會。儘管這樣的企圖心受到了美國以亞太經濟合作會議的運行機制的阻撓，以2011年11月在歐巴馬總統出生地夏威夷檀香山的APEC會議為例，最為明顯感到美國重返亞洲的戰略已經發生作用。在歐巴馬上台後，逐漸從伊拉克和阿富汗撤軍，而將外交戰略轉到亞太地區，中國因南海爭議首當其衝成為美國箭靶。

2008年7月，在日本北海道洞爺湖溫泉舉行「八大」工業國首腦會議時，金磚四國（巴西，俄羅斯，印度，中國）領導人在會議期間，俄羅斯總統梅德維傑夫，中國國家主席胡錦濤，印度總理辛格和巴西總統路易斯伊納西奧盧拉達席爾瓦，首次以四國領導人共同會晤的形式出現，奠定了未來金磚國家領導者領袖高峰會的機制。2008年9月，「金磚四國」外長在俄羅斯葉卡捷琳堡舉行會議，就氣候變化、能源及糧食安全等問題進行了討論。同年11月，「金磚四國」財政部長在巴西聖保羅舉行會議，呼籲改革國際金融體系。2009年6月16日，「金磚四國」峰會在俄羅斯葉卡捷琳堡舉行，這成為「金磚四國」的首次正式峰會。2010年4月15日，第二屆「金磚四國」峰會在巴西首都巴西利亞舉行。2011年4月14日，第三屆「金磚國家領袖」峰會在中國海南省三亞舉行，南非首次獲邀加入並首次出席會議。BRICKS（Brazil, Russia, India, China, South Africa），構成了金磚五國跨越亞非拉的國際經濟合作的領袖高峰會。同年，莫斯科國立國際關係大學成立了金磚國家研究中心，11月9-10日並進行研討會廣泛討論，同時在俄羅斯世界和平基金會的倡議下，總統府設置了金磚國家委員會，莫斯科國立國際關係大學多位學者都是其中成員。由此窺知，俄羅斯擴大國際影響力與提高國內生活水準的長期國家戰略目標已經浮現。2012年3月29日第四屆「金磚國家領袖」峰會則在印度新德里舉行。

金磚國家人口占了全世界人口的45%，陸地面積30%，世界生產總量25%，占了全球生產總量成長的50%。政治大學俄羅斯研究所教授王定士的看法和俄羅斯八大工業集團代表盧科夫（Вадим ЛУКОВ）相同，認為金磚國家可以發揮影響國際秩序的影響力，主要是在聯合國安全理事會常任理事國的架構下影響國際安全議題並且發揮決策性的力量。俄羅斯方面認為金磚國家是以世界經濟秩序重建的改革者聯盟姿態出現，對世界政策具有發言和影響作用。

2009-2012金磚國家的對內生產總值動態變化與歐美參照

（в % к предыдущему году; 2011-2012 гг. –預測）

	2010	2011	2012
巴西	7,5	4,5	4,1
俄羅斯	4,0	4,8	4,5
印度	10,4	8,2	7,8
中國	10,3	9,8	9,5
南非	2,8	3,5	3,8
美國	2,8	2,8	2,9
歐元區	1,7	1,6	1,8

Источник: IMF World Economic Outlook, April 2011.

　　俄羅斯經濟研究院院長格林別爾格（Гринберг Р.С.）認為，蘇聯解體後俄羅斯生活在震撼的陰影下，許多轉型國家都是越來越好取得經濟成果，俄羅斯卻因為轉型陷入動盪和貧困，這樣的劇變深深刺激了俄羅斯人的心靈和社會意識，俄羅斯經濟落後於先進發達的工業國家，但是俄羅斯是科技、武器和人文思想的大國，這種經濟環境不對稱的痛苦在俄羅斯心理上造成傷害，俄羅斯是好於奉獻所能的國家，金磚國家的結合給俄羅斯找到了可發揮的平台。

伊凡諾夫斯基（Ивановский З.В）認為，許多國際媒體負面評價金磚國家的組合，認為金磚國家之間有文化傳統上的差異，彼此之間還有領土爭議以及貿易競爭關係，因此很難整合出共同意見。僅管國際媒體看法消極和嘲諷金磚國家難成氣候，不過這些國家都是區域的一極，符合他們追求國際多極化政策並且反對美國單極的國際軍事霸權以及西方經濟壟斷現狀。對於美國國防力量的擴充以及北約東擴和導彈防禦系統的設置都感受到威脅，從國際安全角度來看金磚國家具有共識。

俄羅斯遠東科學院院長契塔連科（Титаренко М.Л.）認為，中印俄都是文明大國，這種三角合作關係早存在於俄羅斯的高層當中。金磚國家之間的聯盟關係儘管困難重重，但具有搭建與美國平等對話平台的正面意涵，也是一個建立國際新秩序的合作機制，中印俄三國的學術研究單位早已經建立研究合作關係，他認為俄羅斯有很豐富的外交傳統文化與外交經驗，可以對金磚國家在國際舞台中建立對話機制很有幫助。中國俄羅斯研究專家、廣州暨南大學國際傳播研究中心主任吳非教授對筆者表示，俄羅斯文明與外交將成為能源大國到科技大國的過渡期，是俄羅斯在過渡期的外交策略。

二、俄羅斯強化全球佈局的能力

俄羅斯外長拉夫羅夫2010年9月21日在聯合國千年發展目標峰會上表示，全球發展與安全問題息息相關，經濟問題所引發社會問題包括疾病、低收入戶的增加、失控移民和恐怖主義蔓延都會導致全球經濟危機。經濟危機成為安全危機的關鍵因素。

俄羅斯智庫「團結以俄羅斯為名」（Единство во имя России）副總裁托羅亞（Георгий Толорая）在一篇名為「俄羅斯與金磚國家：互動戰略」的文章中指出：金磚國家將改變世界經濟與政治樣貌，俄羅斯應制訂國家長期發展的對外經濟戰略和政治戰略目標並且在這些金磚國家集團中找到自己定位。

　　他認為金磚國家集團在國際秩序中扮演越來越有影響力的角色，俄羅斯不應該把金磚國家當作對抗西方集團的一極，因為俄羅斯在歷史文明方面是傾向於西方文明的，俄羅斯要追求更公平的世界分配權力，不論在國際貨幣基金組織中的決定權或是國際原材料價格的制訂方面，應該讓金磚國家有更多的發言權，俄羅斯應該扮演金磚國家間不同利益的協調者，扮演南北與東西方國家之間的橋梁，以合作取代對抗西方集團的兩極化意識形態對立概念，作為俄羅斯參與國際影響力的思想基礎。俄羅斯應該朝著積極正面的方向使金磚國家發揮影響世界政策的作用，包括以下幾個方面：

第一、創造更民主與公平的國際經濟財經體系。

第二、形成更緊密外交聯繫的網絡關係影響世界政治領域。

第三、在聯合國安理會架構下發展合作關係。

第四、金磚國家作為一個合作機制，發展與其他國際組織包括聯合國、上海合作組織、歐亞經濟合作組織的互動關係，把印尼、埃及、墨西哥納入未來合作的成員國名單。

第五、強化技術科技的合作關係作為經濟社會現代化的基礎以改善人民生活水準。

俄羅斯輿論界認為金磚國家成員都是地區大國，對於區域間整合發揮著帶領的作用，俄羅斯可在電力、航天航空、健康保險、生物燃料以及奈米技術方面有更多的投資。托羅拉亞認為，俄羅斯應該以外交模式強化金磚國家在安全議題方面的合作，使其扮演國家安全方面更重要的角色。

　　從以上看，俄羅斯並不會被某一個集團或是組織所困死，不會被與西方對立的立場所限制，不容易同中國成為其他國家的箭靶或是針對的目標，俄羅斯在能源和軍事的優勢下，可以來回於不同組織中達到他的靈活外交關係和聯繫協調的關鍵作用。俄羅斯比中國似乎更為明智和務實。俄羅斯在全球發展戰略中強調安全的重要性，並且試圖把金磚國家作為與其他組織之間的對話基礎，強化俄羅斯在不同集團國家之間的橋梁和協調作用，以此發揮俄羅斯聯繫和溝通的影響力，降低俄羅斯被孤立與圍堵的可能性，來達到擴大參與國際事務的全球治理能力。未來俄羅斯將以綿密的外交手段和建立國際組織之間的合作網路關係，提升俄羅斯的全球佈局能力，使俄羅斯在國際上更加利於不敗之地。托羅拉亞也是俄羅斯世界和平基金會的亞洲部主任，掌管亞洲、非洲和拉丁美洲的俄羅斯文化和俄語推廣的事務，該基金會主導協助在總統府架構下設置了金磚國家委員會，把俄羅斯文化和語言的推廣與俄羅斯外交聯繫在一起，讓更多國家的人學習俄語，作為俄羅斯思想輸出、建立友俄人士以及執行在這些地區強化俄羅斯影響力的基礎工作。

三、俄羅斯全球發展戰略特點

俄羅斯科學院世界經濟和國際關係研究所一份《2030全球戰略預測》報告指出：通過強化俄羅斯的國際地位和增強俄羅斯對世界進程和全球治理的影響，以提高俄羅斯人民的生活品質。幾方面論點：

第一、大國協商更為關鍵：安全與發展問題的全球化將使主要大國的政治精英的戰略思維發生變化。強化本國作為「力量中心」之一的任務將會轉變為另一個，即行使「負責任大國」之能力，以應對共同的安全與發展挑戰。大國關係的特點將是：在全球安全和發展問題上進行合作，並在選擇這些問題的解決方案時於自利的知覺中開展競爭，但結合與其他大國的協商。

第二、全球治理意識取代對立意識形態：意識形態將更頻繁地與全球的政治、社會經濟和文化發展趨勢相關聯，而非僅僅集中於不同國家的內部政治生活。這將成為未來全球治理意識形態的基礎。全球化意識形態與此前一樣，仍將面臨攻擊性、排外和孤立主義思潮的對立。這種對抗的結果取決於某一團體在不同層面上建設性地組織其社會與政治力量的能力。一種認識正在全球範圍內擴展，即大部分的國家發展和安全問題需全球或地區層面的參與。在未來二十年，平等思想和與此相關的對於社會公平的新解讀將流行起來並頗具影響。

第三、全球治理的機制和原則將繼續形成：超國家經濟政治
　　　治理的綜合性機構2030年前將不會明確定型。但以正式
　　　的和非正式的、傳統的和新起的國際機制為基礎，將
　　　初步形成建立全球治理體系某些要素的穩定趨勢。向全
　　　球制度化進程開放的領域有：知識產權、金融、國際
　　　貿易、能源及大宗商品、海空運輸管理、世界勞動力
　　　市場、防止大規模殺傷性武器的擴散、維和及解決衝
　　　突、打擊國際恐怖主義及販毒、保障海運安全與打擊海
　　　盜、與貧困和流行病鬥爭、消除自然災害後果以及氣候
　　　變化。建立旨在保護文化遺產、生物多樣性和某些生態
　　　系統的全球監控機構的計畫將得以推進。

第四、世界經濟發展的主要動力為創新和全球化：世界金融經
　　　濟危機的影響將體現在證券市場的波狀震盪中，以及由
　　　發展中和發達經濟體雙速發展（two-speed growth）導致
　　　的宏觀經濟不平衡的風險持續存在。反危機措施中包括
　　　了經濟結構現代化、建立新的技術平臺、人力資源投資
　　　等。在未來二十年，世界經濟增長整體上不會受到資源
　　　保障（原料、勞動力、資本和技術）方面的制約。但個
　　　別地區將飽受此類問題的困擾。

第五、社會矛盾不僅會侵蝕一些國家的社會體系，還會招致一
　　　系列國際社會問題（移民、人口、種族衝突等）。引起
　　　全球社會爆炸的不是「世界窮人」，而是那部分對其內
　　　部社會分層不斷擴大感到最不快的中產階級。

第六、國際安全體系：世界大國在維護世界和平上相互協作的
　　　趨勢將壓倒相互對抗的趨勢。軍事建設和軍備發展將會

繼續。但與此相關的相互猜疑，至少部分地，將被創建新的全球安全維護機制、採取信任措施和共同發展武器系統予以平衡。主要趨勢是在對外政策中借助於下列工具，擴大「軟實力」和「巧實力」的運用：金融和經濟優勢；科技進步；文化與教育；擴大意識形態的影響。

第七、俄羅斯的風險和機遇：未來二十年，為避免自身不被邊緣化、能應對未來的風險，以及利用全球化所帶來的新機遇，俄羅斯必須使自己的內外戰略有效地適應全球發展的主要趨勢。在社會領域方面，如何改革現行的社會制度，並在改革中避免由於功能削弱而自身受損的官僚機構與需要有效的官僚機構的社會之間的衝突。這不僅需要政治意志，還需要實實在在地擴大公民社會的活動領域。在對外政策方面，在表達俄羅斯對外政策利益和制訂對外政策戰略時，如何克服或限制傳統上把美國和中國作為潛在對手的認識。改變俄羅斯內部強大利益集團不參與國際雙邊談判的消極態度。

四、俄羅斯政經問題與前景

莫斯科高等經濟研究院院長亞辛認為，俄羅斯在近十餘年已經邁入發達國家的經濟行列，蘇聯解體前夕與解體之後的問題不在於依賴能源和原材料的出口，而在於經濟結構的管理失衡，過去包括商品短缺，供需結構不平衡，物流機制欠缺，政治鬥爭等因素。俄羅斯需要更加穩定的金融機制和貸款政策，減少政府對於商業的過度干涉，保持政府與企業之間有效溝通，才能維持俄羅斯吸引外資投入的興趣。

儘管如此，根據中國社科院的一份研究報告顯示，兩千年以後俄羅斯出口石油和天然氣的比重仍然在出口項目中的一半，這樣的比重還在增加，普京執政以來，國家加強了對經濟的調控力度。主要措施為：一是把加速經濟發展作為實現強國戰略的主要內容。為此普京在2003年提出經濟翻番的目標，之後不斷強調要盡一切努力實現這一目標；二是在財稅、投資、匯率與貨幣領域加強調控力度；三是政府通過各種經濟發展綱要，指導經濟發展；四是加強國家對戰略資源部門的控制，掌握國家經濟命脈。俄羅斯石油公司對尤甘斯克石油天然氣公司的收購，俄羅斯天然氣工業股份公司對西伯利亞石油公司的收購，均是這一政策的具體體現。這些舉措提高了國家對戰略資源的控制能力。另外還通過制定自然資源領域的法律法規加強對戰略資源的控制。科研投入仍然不足以維繫發展高科技產業，醫療、教育、住宅和農業的四大國家優先計畫，仍依賴政府去負擔，俄羅斯政府承擔社會福利的能力仍然受到經濟條件的限制，俄羅斯的社會化政策仍然需要靠能源收入來維繫，地區的不平衡與收入差距的擴大化短期仍無法有效解決。

金磚國家也試圖在國際政治態度上產生影響力。2011年11月24日，金磚國家副外長在莫斯科舉行聯合會議，共同發表聲明譴責敘利亞的暴力衝突，公開呼籲各方尊重中東國家主權獨立和領土完整，以和平方式開展廣泛對話，解決危機。敘利亞繼續暴力鎮壓反政府示威者。聯合國估計自反政府抗議爆發以來，已有3500多人死亡。十月，中俄兩國還在聯合國會議上否決了西方國家起草制裁敘利亞的提案。不過俄羅斯過度干涉在國際問題採取平衡西方國家的政治立場，也會招致西方國家的報復，比如對於俄羅斯2011年12月4日的國會選舉舞弊的抗議操作，相關監測選舉過程多是西方的非政府組織。在2012總統前哨戰的俄羅斯國會選舉，下議院國家杜馬俄羅斯統一團結黨的席位就下降了百分之十五，共計450個杜馬議席，統一俄羅斯黨贏得238席，占了52.88%，比2007年的315席少了77席。俄羅斯研究者吳非教授就曾在2011年1月22日的鳳凰衛視節目中表示，普京和梅德維傑夫之間有過多的重疊和相似度，普京未來要獲得絕對多數民意就必須有俄共的支持，俄共在2011年國家杜馬選舉中獲得92席，佔了20.46%，增加了35席，約增加上升了7.63%的席次。反映了梅德維傑夫退出總統選舉的效應，也為普京重返總統大位增加了與反對黨之間協商的必要性。

五、俄羅斯未來發展目標

總體而言，俄羅斯應會在幾方面做出努力：

第一、強化區域合作與落實全球多極國際主義政策：俄羅斯藉由金磚國家高峰會議組織新型國際政經聯盟，落實俄羅斯多極化國際體系政策，實為尋求國際聯盟者，以期抵制美國國防的擴充以及北約組織東擴下進行佈署導彈防禦系統對俄羅斯國家安全構成的威脅。俄羅斯將以金磚國家的經濟實力提高自身國際的發言權和國際地位，企圖強化聯合國安理會的國際軍事安全議題的決策作用。美俄又在國際競逐構成了分庭抗禮的趨勢特點。

第二、改善官僚腐化結構：俄羅斯的官僚體系中存在為少數利益者服務的偏頗觀念，尤其在銀行體系中存在許多障礙和欠缺服務的觀念，儘管減少了許多不必要的舞弊，與替主子掌管錢袋的官僚思想，卻給廣大民眾產生了負面觀感，造成銀行服務不佳與協調效率低下的問題，這會在國際金融與經濟合作中令他國退卻。官僚體系也養成眾人不作為的惰性以及保守專制的習氣，很難產生活絡經濟與帶動企業升騰的正面氣氛，導致了企業對政府國際化的消極態度以及民眾對政府執政負面的形象觀感。

第三、增加與反對派的溝通：儘管只有國家領導者展現了親民的作風，可以在普京支持率為63.6%和支持普京的俄羅斯團結統一黨49.29%的差距看出端倪。2011年12月4日舉行的國家杜馬選舉。共計450個杜馬議席全部由公民投票產生。根據公布的結果，統一俄羅斯黨贏得238席，比2007年的315席少了77席。而另外的三個政黨俄羅斯聯邦共產黨得到92席，公正俄羅斯黨得到64席，俄羅斯自由民主黨得到56席。其他參選政黨由於未得到7%的門檻而未能進入議會。俄羅斯國會裡面幾乎是中左勢力，沒有右派的聲音，這種絕對的分歧也是引起俄羅斯反對派且主要是右派的示威遊行抗議的主因，尤其以莫斯科原來在葉利欽總統執政時期的右派政府改革成員為最。這種右派反對勢力剛好與新聞業強調監督政府與新聞自由天職的反對派結合起來，不過新聞記者也有天生有同情弱勢的左派思想，如何促使政府顧好社會福利政策，也成為媒體與政府合作的思想基礎。

第四、增加公民參與的社會氛圍：俄羅斯總統將面臨多數民意支持的考驗，未來如何在社會福利政策上有明確的保障以及擴大促進社會參與的進程，都是俄羅斯政府落實民主化與現代化的考驗。不要過度壓制右派的反對聲音，給俄羅斯反對派生存空間也是普京重返克宮的重要任務，這考驗他的社會危機處理能力與視野胸襟的包容力。

第五、增加在第三世界或反美國家中的協調角色：俄羅斯習慣在國際上偏袒與西方國家敵對的國家，儘管俄羅斯好像有了弱勢國家者的庇護者地位，但是往往造成世界觀感不佳，俄羅斯不應該以軍售或是為了爭取國際地位而去支持一些有問題的國家，這樣反而讓俄羅斯以合作取代對抗的國家安全戰略受到打擊，俄羅斯應該以本國民意為優先考量，去決定國際處理的態度與外交方針，這樣可以減少政府忽略民意又過度干涉國際政治反而招致西方國家報復的被動情況。

第六、推廣俄羅斯語言和文化：俄羅斯從自身的文化與傳統中找到自信，同時俄羅斯具有豐富的外交傳統和經驗，金磚國家給俄羅斯提供很好的表演舞台和貢獻經驗的空間。俄羅斯學界和政府或是非政府組織團結力量，重建俄羅斯自信和光榮。這個概念可以從總統府下設的俄羅斯世界和平基金會一方面參與文化語言推廣，一方面參與金磚國家聯盟的勢力看出。

第七、能源作為國際制衡與合作的外交戰略：俄羅斯將以更全
　　　面開放的態度參與國際事務，擺脫俄羅斯在國際上孤
　　　立和自私的負面形象，以文化交流和國際合作的方式
　　　取代消極對抗的傳統意識形態，改善官僚體制不作為或
　　　是亂作為給國家發展所帶來的障礙，提高俄羅斯公民參
　　　與公共事務的能力以提升國家民主體制中存在的官僚問
　　　題。藉由國際參與達到俄羅斯經濟成長改善人民生活水
　　　準的目的。金磚國家的機制是俄羅斯展現跨國協調能力
　　　的開始，全球化為俄羅斯帶來的機遇，但俄羅斯不希望
　　　能源成為全球化下的犧牲品，能源只是參與國際經濟秩
　　　序的重要手段來提升俄羅斯全面參與國際事務的全球佈
　　　局能力。

第八、擴大參與亞洲政治與經濟的影響力：俄羅斯主導金磚五
　　　國聯盟顯然展現在亞洲影響中國和印度的架勢。蘇聯
　　　解體之後，俄羅斯的地緣戰略受到美國為首的北大西
　　　洋公約組織東擴的公開排擠；中國則利用上海合作組織
　　　中俄羅斯的不作為，對中亞地區進行侵蝕，和美國一
　　　樣企圖繞過俄羅斯取得對中亞各國石油與天然氣的優
　　　勢。沒想到中亞國家從軍事到政治經濟無不依賴俄羅斯
　　　的幫助，俄羅斯經過普京執政八年後，鞏固獨聯體主
　　　要是中亞地區的政策獲得落實與成功。在2008年5月梅
　　　德維傑夫正式就任總統之後，8月面對喬治亞對於外高
　　　加所地區南奧塞梯自治共和國首府茨欣瓦利市的軍事入
　　　侵，採取主動回擊，改變原來蘇聯解體後俄羅斯－喬治
　　　亞－南奧塞梯三國為避免軍事衝突所組建的聯合維和部

隊的局面，俄羅斯全面主導了南奧塞梯自治共和國的軍隊並正式承認了該國的主權與獨立。中國由於自身陷於新疆、西藏與台灣問題上，片面認為南奧塞梯的問題是喬治亞的內部問題，狹隘地認為俄羅斯支持了喬治亞的分離主義，故沒有像其他上海合作組織的中亞成員國支持俄羅斯的軍事行動，尤其2008年8月8日，北京正在舉辦奧運開幕，對於俄羅斯沒有遵照奧運期間停戰的作為很不諒解。不過中國這次的決策是失誤的，也可以說是傲慢的。因為俄羅斯未來在亞洲政策與對上合組織的態度上，會對中國相對的冷淡。台灣可爭取俄羅斯的支持，對台灣增加國際空間是非常有幫助的！在未來亞洲戰略上還是美俄的競逐，中國已經在2012年的政權交接時刻選擇向俄羅斯靠攏。

參考文獻

1. Obama: China must 'play by the rules', The Washington Post, November 13.

   http://www.washingtonpost.com/world/obama-at-apec-summit-china-must-play-by-the-rules/2011/11/12/gIQALRu2FN_story.html

2. Obama heads to Asia focused on China's power, the Washington Post, November 11.

3. http://www.mid.ru/brics.nsf/WEBforumBric

4. Вадим ЛУКОВ, БРИКС-ФАКТОР ГЛОБАЛЬНОГО ЗНАЧЕНИЯ.

   http://www.mid.ru/brics.nsf/WEBforumBric/E0A80FB2A260663 3C32578DC00482A08

5. Гринберг Р.С. Экономика России в посткризисном мире: варианты адаптации в контексте БРИК

   http://www.mid.ru/brics.nsf/WEBforumBric/5A5C84BE5297388 1C3257859005A82B0

6. Ивановский З.В. БРИК в зеркале мировой печати .

   http://www.mid.ru/brics.nsf/WEBforumBric/CD2BDDEE91327C 4FC3257859005A82A5

7. Титаренко М.Л. БРИК: предпосылки взаимодействия, подходы и оценки сторон

   http://www.mid.ru/brics.nsf/WEBforumBric/6D55AB0FA4BF25B 6C3257859005A82B1

8. https://visit.un.org/chinese/News/fullstorynews. asp?newsID=14121

9. Георгий Толорая (2011). Россия и БРИКС: стратегия взаимодействия，Журнал Стратегия России, №8, Август 2011. http://www.gazetaprotestant.ru/2011/09/rossiya-i-briks-strategiya-vzaimodejstviya/

10. http://www.imemo.ru/ru/publ/2011/forecasts/PrognozReady_ CH_03.pdf

11. 俄國：從深重的危機走向市場經濟 http://www.bbc.co.uk/zhongwen/trad/business/2011/11/111129_ russia.shtml

12. 邢廣程主編，俄羅斯經濟的特點、問題與前景，《2006年：俄羅斯東歐中亞國家發展報告》，社會科學文獻出版社2007年4月版。 http://euroasia.cass.cn/news/60306.htm

13. 金磚國家敦促敘利亞當局與反對派談判 http://www.bbc.co.uk/zhongwen/trad/world/2011/11/111125_ brics_syria.shtml

14. http://archive.kremlin.ru/text/news/2008/07/203878.shtml

俄羅斯思想轉折下的

衝突與和諧

俄羅斯從立國以來始終面臨外敵入侵的命運，然而俄羅斯在戰爭洗禮後卻是愈發變得益常的堅毅與冷靜：磨難使他們深沉，宗教使他們偉大。俄羅斯只要被侵略一次，它的領土就要擴張一次，這樣的結果是令他國省思的。愈挫愈勇是這個國家民族的特徵，俄羅斯是獨特而不容侵犯的國家。近代俄羅斯經歷了拿破崙入侵、兩次世界大戰以及冷戰體系瓦解後的國家社會巨變。俄羅斯的心理層面發生了變化，一種衝突與和諧的極端思想震盪使俄羅斯社會變得更加混亂不安與不可預測，這種思想的轉折與外在的威脅和內部的衝突下更加鮮明，期盼和平與和諧的理念變得愈加的奢侈和困難。

一、俄羅斯的思想轉折特點

十九世紀初，拿破崙入侵俄國之後，掀起了俄羅斯知識份子反專制的風潮，也使得俄羅斯民族主義得到興起，把陀斯妥耶夫斯基與托爾斯泰等諸多的俄羅斯文學家與哲學家推向了開創俄羅斯精神文明的前列，也把俄羅斯精神文明推向了世界的舞台。如同俄羅斯成為共產主義國家的發源地與實踐者，凡此皆與俄羅斯文化傳統有密切的關係。可以說俄羅斯文明的創造來自於蒙昧無知；宗教精神的追求來自於迷信專制，從無到有的過程證明俄羅斯人的學習和創造能力，從有到無的過程證明俄國人自我摧毀和反思的個性。在1861年亞歷山大二世沙皇解除農奴制度以前，俄羅斯這片廣大的領土還是農奴與專制階層的沃土。如同政治上的沙皇專制，宗教上的東正教會屬於國家階層的一部分，許多地方上的封建地主自己就蓋教堂，聘用的教士基本素質與文化涵養不高，教會發展史就是少數統治階層的一部分，政教之間的分裂與衝突也多半圍繞在統治權歸屬的問題，不論屬於國家的東正教會或是被排斥在政教合一制度外的神秘異教，俄羅斯十九世紀末以前的宗教整體普遍缺乏真正意義上的精神內涵在裡面。

陀斯妥耶夫斯基與托爾斯泰的宗教精神僅管來自於信仰上帝，但是與教會的控制與形體無關，而是發自內心對於人類乃至於對俄羅斯人民苦難命運的一種憐憫與關懷。也就是當十九世紀中葉以來，俄羅斯社會主義追求者，在反對專制的行列中也反對了那種控制人民思想的教會，共產主義對無產階級的底層而言是一種嚮往，當蘇維埃政權在提倡無神論時，在某種程度是反對原來屬於沙皇政教合一底下的教會特權，這一點使它在同情底層人民的俄羅斯知識份子當中得到了支持。同樣地，俄羅斯廣大底層的苦難工農當中，他們原來對於宗教上的迷信多過於對東正教的教規與教義的遵守或理解。這樣一來，宗教教會成為了與沙皇專制同樣的意涵，是控制人民思想與財產的壓迫者，布爾什維克黨在以無神論摧毀過往屬於俄羅斯專制的教會特權時得到了基礎，取而代之的是人民對於共產主義的狂熱與崇拜，信仰共產主義成為人民的另一個宗教，人民的無知不論在帝制或共和國時期都是一樣的，俄羅斯知識份子的革命行為是痛心之後對人民苦難命運的抗爭。史達林的鎮壓與清洗摧毀了俄羅斯精神文化，逃離蘇聯的知識份子把俄羅斯的精神文明推向國外。

蘇聯解體後，宗教得到了自由，俄羅斯人民的意識形態領域獲得了解放，各類宗教隨之填補這樣的信仰真空狀態。俄羅斯的總統葉利欽與普京與東正教牧首的合作關係到像是俄羅斯的雙頭鷹標幟，恢復俄羅斯昔日光榮的政治象徵意涵大於實際的意識形態操控。今日俄羅斯的文藝復興思潮在銜接十九世紀末到二十世紀初這樣的俄羅斯宗教精神文明的基礎上，使得俄羅斯人逐漸找回自己的自信心，繼續把這樣的俄羅斯獨特精神發光發熱。

以人為核心的世界觀在俄羅斯19世紀具有開創性和奠基性的意義。988年，俄羅斯國家領導人也就是基輔羅斯大公弗拉基米爾把東正教定為國教之後，政教合一的俄羅斯統治者把自己置於君權神授的至高無上地位上，形成了俄羅斯文化中皇權極權化與宗教神權極權化的極權制度特徵。19世界俄羅斯思想家對於反對沙皇極權和反基督的世界體系是有深刻的社會環境因素的，這也註定俄羅斯想要建構的新的人道主義世界觀是擺脫神人二元對立學說而結合神人的新世界觀，也就是俄羅斯的人道世界觀是站在宗教性質辯證思維基礎上的！如何從承認神存在的先驗基礎上走向神人的絕對的、純粹的、崇高的地位，是本文要論述的對象，亦即共產主義思想根源中人性與個體命運的關注是俄羅斯建立宗教虛無主義和人道主義世界觀的核心問題，進而說明共產主義在唯物基礎上是把人從歷史過程中被奴役和損害的工具角色轉換成社會發展的最終目的和服務對象。被譽為「20世紀俄國的黑格爾」的知名偉大俄羅斯思想家別爾嘉耶夫曾說：「別林斯基是俄國共產主義的先驅。他已經肯定地說出布爾什維克的道德。」別林斯基的思想體系可以作為其中一個代表來分析論述。

探究俄羅斯共產主義思想根源的意義在於其崇高的道德出發點。在歷史過程中體制的僵化被視為對人性的扼殺，凡物必經過成、住、壞、空；人必經過生、老、病、死的自然規律。然而，對於人性問題的關注以及把人作為最高意識形態的最終目的卻具有永恆的價值和意義。19世紀俄羅斯許多重要思想家試圖要為人的苦難尋找出口點，要把對人的關懷和慈愛當作純粹和絕對的最高形式，這為俄羅斯建立一套人本主義和人道精神的世界觀奠定了前所未有且具有道德高度的思想體系大廈。

別爾嘉耶夫認為：「斯拉夫主義者走向宗教、走向信仰；西方主義者走向革命，走向社會主義」。不論哪種情況，都是力圖得到整體性和極權性的世界觀，力圖取得哲學與生活的統一，理論與實踐的統一。別爾嘉耶夫認為「俄羅斯虛無主義和共產主義的主題是同一個主題。」別爾嘉耶夫在對比斯拉夫主義者和西方主義者時認為：斯拉夫主義者把俄羅斯農民村社當作一個世界的整體和永恆的基礎，把村社集體和個人主義對立起來，從這點來看斯拉夫主義者是曖昧主義者，但是他們的現在於把俄羅斯民族當作世界的希望以及俄羅斯人有著未來世界的偉大使命，這卻是斯拉夫主義者的貢獻。斯拉主義者的民粹思想深遠地影響著俄羅斯人的世界觀和人生哲學與美學，亦即最美的形式就是俄羅斯人無我奉獻的群體生活，它代表著世界和諧的最高形式和最終目的。

別爾嘉耶夫認為：「別林斯基是19世紀後半葉社會主義的流派代表，是車尼爾雪夫斯基的直接先驅，也是俄國馬克思主義者的直接先驅」別林斯基寫道：「黑格爾，向您的哲學頂尖帽子致敬，但如果要我沿著發展的階梯爬到上層的話，……向您告辭，……我將向下看，如果我的任何兄弟不能安逸的話，我並不嚮往幸福，和才華，……這就是我的世界觀，我將

帶他一同死去。」「對我而言，沉思與感覺，理解與受折磨
——是同一東西。」「主體、個體、個人的命運比世界命運以
及中國皇帝的健康更重要」別爾嘉耶夫評論別林斯基與陀斯妥
也夫斯基創造的伊凡・卡拉馬佐夫主人公所表述的嬰兒的眼淚
與世界和諧之間衝突的辯證法有著驚人的相似」。

　　十九世紀末到二十世紀初，俄羅斯各種力量包括人道主
義者和社會主義者皆對現存體制和環境感到不滿。反體制的革
命力量在社會悲觀的氣氛中摧毀了一切，新的意識形態必須以
積極、樂觀和烏托邦式的理想來建構一個新國家的藍圖，任何
違背此一願景的力量都將被視為敵人而打倒，新的階級對立矛
盾又再產生。

二、戰爭與和平的關係省思

　　俄羅斯許多偉大的文藝作品都是以戰爭為背景的。早在
古羅斯時期，最早的佚名詩歌作品《伊戈爾遠征記》就呼籲俄
羅斯人的團結與反省。1812年拿破崙入侵俄羅斯，以此作為小
說創作體材的有俄羅斯大文豪列夫・托爾斯泰，他的《戰爭與
和平》開創了俄羅斯長篇小說的先河，作品反應了俄羅斯當時
主流社會的特徵，作品兼具史料檔案價值與人文宗教精神。高
爾基曾言：「不認識托爾斯泰者，不可能認識俄羅斯。」在文
學創作和社會活動中，他還提出了「托爾斯泰主義」，對很多
政治運動有著深刻影響。

　　托爾斯泰的《戰爭與和平》不但可以作為歷史資料被保
存下來，作品在精神價值觀上注入了作家最重要的思想，就

是如何對人類和平作出貢獻，他延續了宗教中人卑神尊的態度，提醒人的所作所為都是任何一個歷史事件的非常渺小的部分，集體的破壞力量是違背人本身存在的意義，傷害了人類本身。1812年拿破崙入侵俄羅斯，不但激發了俄羅斯的創作能量，也是俄羅斯在歷史規律中如何總結經驗教訓的經典範本，俄羅斯人對於人類精神價值的經歷和總結都對世界具有莫大的參考與借鑒的價值。

托爾斯泰（1828-1910）在出版他的文學巨作《戰爭與和平》之前寫了一篇作者序，裡面表達作者自己對這部作品的看法。他希望讀者要特別集中注意力關注他要表達的想法，最重要的想法就是「即使最偉大的人物在任何歷史事件中都只有微小的作用，這表示歷史事件是超乎人們智力可以探究的。」如果偉人的作用是微小的，那麼平常人在歷史事件中更是微不足道的，那麼那股具大足以摧毀人類的戰爭力量是如何產生的？人有沒有方法可以抑制這樣集體瘋狂行為的產生？如果偉人和領袖都身不由己，那誰可以控制自己？誰又可以控制戰爭的爆發？

1812年拿破崙入侵俄羅斯這個歷史事件提供了托爾斯泰對「自由意志」命題的分析。如果拿破崙自己也不能算是操控這場戰爭的原因？那麼誰操控了人類彼此大屠殺的戰爭？必定有個高於人的「自由意志」的力量存在？托爾斯泰認為「人的行為越抽象，與他人行為聯繫越少，行為越自由；反之，聯繫越多，我們行為就越不自由。」換言之，像拿破崙這樣的領袖人物「越有對他人最大的支配權，其實也就對別人有最大的依從。」人與人之間的關係似乎是相互牽制的。

俄羅斯思想轉折下的衝突與和諧

從托爾斯泰的觀點來看，人越減少集體組織的聯繫就可以越減少對他人的威脅，也避免自己陷入到不可自拔的錯誤當中，集體的行為舉止通常會變成是瘋狂且缺少理智的。《戰爭與和平》這部作品不但提供了認識俄羅斯當時人物特徵與歷史環境的歷史素材，也提供了人們思索如何獲得自由意志與避免大規模屠殺戰爭發生的線索。至於像是俄羅斯這樣無辜的被侵略者有何應對之措施嗎？如果俄羅斯採取入侵者同樣的舉措，那麼自己就會成為製造戰爭的入侵者；如果不採取支配他人的舉措，又會變成受害者，進退兩難？或許托爾斯泰藉著《戰爭與和平》提出這樣的「自由意志」的命題，可以讓更多人意識到「自由與依從」這樣的關係是如何產生的，以減少因為不以「個人自由意志」為主而做出瘋狂且身不由己的失智行為，例如大規模的入侵戰爭。也因此，俄羅斯一直對集體且大規模的組織抱持有戒心。故托爾斯泰的思想收到了西方的歡迎，俄國內部的自由主義和人道主義者，無疑是西方長期以來拉攏和對抗俄羅斯極端斯拉夫主義和極權主義的對象。

如何避免變成為入侵者或是被入侵者？答案似乎就在認識人的「自由意志」與依從他人之間的關係裡面。我們就可以理解為何「自由」這個命題一直是一個有恆的命題，因為只要有人群關係和組織行為存在，「個人

◆ 托爾斯泰肖像油畫，現存於特列季亞科夫畫廊。

◆托爾斯泰故居的陵園位
　於亞斯納亞－博良納
　（Ясная Поляна）
　（圖片來源：
　http://gooigr.net）

自由意志」的程度就成為了衡量任何組織團體民主程度的指
標。「個人自由意志」越多，殺戮越少，民主成分越多。同樣
地，任何與他人關係只要發生殺戮與傷害存在，就絕對不可能
有「個人自由意志」的存在，因為「自由意志」是不能與他人
發生聯繫的，就甭提傷害他人與集體殺戮了。所以人越減少對
他人的支配行為就越獲得自由的意志。「自由意志」是一種自
我要求與自我行為的負責，是和平的基礎。和平是有賴於每個
人的自我要求，控制別人只能產生不自由與發生衝突；換言
之，「自由意志」是和平的基礎。戰爭是「自由意志」的失
控表現，和平是「自由意志」的發揮結果，「自由意志」的
產生端賴於自我要求的行為完成且不仰賴與支配他人，這應該
是托爾斯泰想表達的想法。托爾斯泰雖然表達了個人相對於
集體是渺小且無力的道德觀，但卻賦予了自由和平的價值。任
何試圖從集體力量中得到支配和操控的權力，只能造成無法控
制的悲劇。

戰爭給俄羅斯人帶來許多創作
的靈感。俄羅斯文藝作品以1812年拿
破崙入侵為體材的還有柴可夫斯基的
音樂作品——《1812序曲》。《1812
序曲》（降E大調序曲「1812」，作
品第49號）是柴可夫斯基於1880年創
作的一部管弦樂作品。為了紀念1812
年庫圖佐夫帶領俄國人民擊退拿破崙
大軍的入侵，贏得俄法戰爭的勝利。
該作品以曲中的炮火聲聞名，在一些
演出中——尤其是戶外演出——曾啟
用真的大炮。該序曲於1882年8月20
日在莫斯科救世主大教堂首演。

俄羅斯浪漫樂派作曲家，其作
品也有一定的民族樂派特徵。其風格
直接和間接地影響了很多後來者。

◆ 米哈伊爾‧庫圖佐夫
（Михаи́л Илларио́нович
Голени́щев-Куту́зов，
1745年9月16日－1813
年4月28日），俄國元
帥，著名將領，軍事家，
1812年曾率領俄國軍隊
擊退拿破崙的大軍，取得
俄法戰爭的勝利。（圖片
引自中文維基百科網）

◆ 彼得‧伊里奇‧柴可夫斯基（Пётр Ильич
Чайковский，1840年5月7日－1893年11月6
日），俄羅斯浪漫樂派作曲家，其作品也有一定
的民族樂派特徵。其風格直接和間接地影響了很
多後來者。1893年，在首演第六號交響曲《悲
愴》九天後，柴可夫斯基死於聖彼得堡的家中。
有些音樂學家（如Milton Cross及David Ewen）
認為，柴可夫斯基對於死亡早有覺悟，而第六
號交響曲正是他寫給自己的安魂曲。著名的創
作還有芭蕾舞劇《天鵝湖》（1876年）、《睡
美人》（1889年）、《胡桃鉗》（1892年）；
以俄羅斯偉大的詩人作家著作創作的歌劇《葉
甫蓋尼‧奧涅金》（1879年）、《黑桃皇后》
（1891年）。（圖片引自中文維基百科網）

1893年，在首演第六號交響曲《悲愴》九天後，柴可夫斯基死於聖彼得堡的家中。有些音樂學家（如Milton Cross及David Ewen）認為，柴可夫斯基對於死亡早有覺悟，而第六號交響曲正是他寫給自己的安魂曲。著名的創作還有芭蕾舞劇《天鵝湖》（1876年）、《睡美人》（1889年）、《胡桃鉗》（1892年）；以俄羅斯偉大的詩人作家著作創作的歌劇《葉甫蓋尼·奧涅金》（1879年）、《黑桃皇后》（1891年）。

俄羅斯在對抗外敵入侵之後，會建造大教堂來紀念抗戰成功。救世主大教堂位於莫斯科，是世界上最高的東正教教堂。該教堂是拿破崙戰爭後，在1812年12月25日由沙皇亞歷山大一世下令修建的，其目的是為了感謝救世主基督「將俄羅斯從失敗中拯救出來，使她避免蒙羞」，並紀念在戰爭中犧牲的俄羅斯人民。

在戰勝拿破崙戰爭之後，俄羅斯沙皇亞歷山大一世下令建造救世主大教堂，救世主大教堂的建造工作於1837年開始，主體結構至1860年基本完工。完成內部豪華的裝飾和壁畫又花費了約20年的時間。1883年5月26日，在沙皇亞歷山大三世加冕的同一天，救世主大教堂正式竣工。救世主大教堂此後成為俄羅斯乃至世界上最大的東正教教堂之一，並成為全俄羅斯東正教普世大牧首的主教堂。1912年，在教堂東門外舉行了亞歷山大三世銅像的落成儀式。

早在十一世紀基輔公國時間，基輔大公智者雅羅斯拉夫在打敗佩徹涅格人的入侵之後，建造了基輔聖索菲雅大教堂。2011年9月24日，基輔聖索菲亞大教堂建成千年慶典在烏克蘭首都基輔舉行。當天，烏克蘭舉行基輔聖索菲亞大教堂建成千年慶典。基輔的聖索菲亞大教堂是東正教最早、最傑出的教堂之一，又是俄羅斯與烏克蘭歷史共同源頭和東正教歷史的見證者，在烏克蘭的文化發展中佔據著重要意義。1990年該教堂作為文化遺產被列入《世界遺產名錄》。

◆ 1817年救世主大教堂鋪設的樣貌（圖片引自俄羅斯維基百科網）

◆ 1881年救世主大教堂的樣貌
（圖片引自俄羅斯維基百科網）

◆ 1931年救世主大教堂被摧毀

俄羅斯再次崛起？——雙頭鷹的亞太政策與戰略思想

◆ 2000年重建後的救世主大教堂（Храм Христа Спасителя）（圖片引自俄羅斯維基百科網）

◆ 聖索菲亞大教堂（圖片引自中文維基百科網）

◆ 聖瓦西里大教堂（Собор Василия Блаженного）（圖片引自中文維基百科網）

又如俄羅斯首都紅場上標致性建築——聖瓦西里大教堂，由9個洋蔥形圓頂組成的多穹頂教堂，屋頂的色彩繽紛，被稱為「用石頭描繪的童話」，中央主樓高達47公尺。這座教堂的興建源於伊凡四世（恐怖者伊凡）於1552年征服了喀山汗國，1556年又征服了阿斯特拉罕汗國（均由蒙古後裔建立），版圖

◆ 俄羅斯政治中心的莫斯科核心建築──克里姆
林宮於1990年被聯合國教科文組織列入為世界
文化遺產（圖片引自中文維基百科網）

到裏海和高外索地區。此後的俄羅斯得以橫越烏拉山往東部向
西伯利亞的區發展。此後俄羅斯逐漸擴張成為了橫跨歐亞大陸
的帝國。為了彰顯豐功偉業，伊凡四世下令修建美侖美奐、華
麗炫目的「面紗大教堂」，1588年，費奧多爾・伊萬諾維奇沙
皇以東正教聖者瓦西里之名，易名為「聖瓦西里教堂」。傳說
伊凡四世甚至下令弄瞎建築師的眼睛，只為了使其不能在建
造出同樣美麗的建築。伊凡四世的殘忍和功績都讓人想起史達
林。史達林的功績在於使國家邁入現代化過程中打敗了德國的
侵略，使國家免於滅亡的災難，瓦解了官僚體系和建立了俄國
長期發展的戰略思想方針。

　　自988年基輔羅斯大公弗拉基米爾把東正教定為國家以
來，俄羅斯人民的生活就與東正教堂密不可分，當初基輔羅斯
大公用強迫受洗的方式推行東正教為國教，儘管正負兩極評價

◆ 莫斯科克里姆宮林內教堂廣場上的聖母升天
教堂（Успенский собор）建於1479年，這
裡舉行沙皇加冕儀式和各種宗教法事。（圖
片來源：http://blog.kp.ru）

不一，但是教堂林立到現在已經成為俄羅斯街景的一部分，早
上人們經常聽到附近教堂傳來的鐘響聲，縱然人生不如意之
事十之八九，那種劃破寧靜清晨的聲響給人們一天帶來了希
望，頗有古人暮鼓晨鐘的啟示意涵。

三、當前極端現象的反思

蘇聯解體之後，冷戰宣告終結，然而西方對於俄羅斯的戰
略圍堵與蔑視的敵對情緒只是更加輕車熟路地加速了，這樣帶

有冷戰性質的「反俄」情緒並沒有隨著冷戰國際體系的瓦解而消失，西方國家戰略圍堵在北約東擴的政策下要使俄羅斯徹底無法成為西方的威脅。蘇聯解體之後，俄羅斯如何重新建立與前蘇聯國家之間的政經關係成為棘手問題，包括邊防安全與海關稅率都是潛藏影響俄羅斯社會秩序與國家安全的動盪因素。振興俄羅斯經濟問題首當其衝解決的就是國家安全問題，俄羅斯貨物通道的正常化與海關和檢警的改革是聯繫在一起的，這些問題都是俄羅斯社會安全問題的根本問題，國家安全問題也是普京上任之後所有改革的基礎。俄羅斯政府與軍檢體系高層中有許多高加索族裔，而同樣地俄羅斯底層的集貨市場也是由高加索族裔把持。因此俄羅斯政府始終將民族分離主義和恐怖主義區隔開來，小心處理社會安全問題也是解決民族分離問題的核心。

　　1991年12月26日蘇聯正式解體後，俄羅斯體制全面轉軌，快速向西方三權分立的立憲民主體制與自由市場經濟體制接軌。戈巴契夫在1985-1991年進行政治「重組」改革之後，強調「公開性」與「新思維」，解除了蘇聯意識形態與蘇聯共黨的專政機制；葉利欽總統接續了民主派改革的作為，1992年以蓋達爾建議的「休克療法」（「震撼療法」）進行經濟體制轉軌走向全面的市場化與私有化。包括俄羅斯在內的前蘇聯加盟共和國的政治與經濟問題全部暴露出來，這些前蘇聯國家對於政治改革失控所造成的經濟崩盤以及社會治安所引發的各種犯罪和貧困問題毫無招架之力。2000年，普京執政之後，必需在既有的體制下進行改革，一種以改善人民生活水準與提高俄羅斯全球治理能力的長期戰略目標逐漸成型，鞏固國家安全成為所有改革的基礎。

經濟改革的結果是盧布貶值與美金市場混亂，俄羅斯進行的市場價格自由化導致了商店貨物不足與物價高漲，開革初期出現了商店貨品短缺，街頭上赤貧的老人沿街乞討或變賣家中的物品，流民和酒鬼經常醉倒街頭而無人理會，民眾身穿便宜次級的服裝和鞋帽，首都街頭似乎愈顯骯髒灰暗，古老美麗的城市籠罩在一片愁雲慘霧的消沉氣氛當中。國際投機客與周邊國家的倒貨者大批湧進莫斯科謀生存，小商小販與貨櫃箱聚集在城市各個市集，販賣便宜的各種家庭生活用品與食品。檯面上銀行家與各類寡頭成為國營企業私有化的第一批受益者，成為俄羅斯人口中的「新俄羅斯權貴」，貧富差距嚴重。

　　這樣權貴參與政治以及民生赤貧的生活景象嚴重打擊了俄羅斯人的信心，心理的創傷很難為外人所理解。此時的俄羅斯人民完全失去人生目標。新興的商業頻道以低俗的影集和政治脫口秀爭取收視率，大家對於媒體中出現的政治鬥爭報導和低俗粗糙的外國暴力影集感到不知所措並且逐漸失去新鮮感而產生厭煩，九十年代的俄羅斯轉型亂象都不是俄羅斯人在蘇聯時期所熟悉的現象，這種陌生的情境與生活的貧困導致了俄國人對於國家喪失信心，民族尊嚴受到嚴重打擊，俄國人在外國人面前更加地感到卑微了。

　　九十年代的反外國情緒表現在一些社會的極端團體的暴力行為上，這是國家與社會失控最先表現出來的一種膚淺情緒，俄羅斯人民並不贊同這種暴力的現象，這種極端暴力也不能簡單被當作為俄羅斯的民族主義或與此劃上等號。但是對於失去民族信心和驕傲的俄國人來說，的確需要有新的意識形態和價值觀來填補社會混亂的思想空白，一種具有民族主義性質的愛國情操，逐漸佔據了俄羅斯公民的意識形態，這種愛國主義對於正在成長的年輕人具有號召力與吸引力。年輕人的愛國熱情開始融化了蘇聯解體後十餘年中所產生的政治冷漠和排斥一切的懷疑情緒。他們成長並生活在普京改革的年代中，開始享受社會物資豐富和國家穩定所帶來的好處，他們無法理解為什麼外國不喜歡俄羅斯和醜化俄羅斯，這樣對保護國家民族使其免於受到欺辱所產生的一種強烈使命感，與普京試圖重振俄羅斯國力與回到國際強權舞台的執政計畫和長遠抱負剛好一拍即合。

普京執政之後，把培養俄羅斯青年當作國家發展戰略的人才目標，為此俄羅斯政府、議會與政黨提供了許多青年參與政策的資源。2000年12月27日，俄羅斯聯邦政府就以1015號決議的形式，批准了「俄羅斯青年」聯邦目標計畫。俄羅斯於2001年和2005年相繼出台了兩個《俄聯邦公民愛國主義教育綱要》。2006年，普京總統批准了《俄羅斯聯邦國家青年政策戰略書》。《至2020年俄聯邦社會經濟長期發展規劃書》指出：「國家青年政策的目的是為青年社會化和自我實現提供條件，發揮青年潛能實行國家的創新發展。」2008年5月，俄羅斯聯邦青年事務署成立。2009年被總統宣佈為「青年年」。

◆ 蘇爾柯夫是普京的智囊，車臣族裔，青年運動的主要金主。蘇爾科夫於今年5月8日遭撤換，一般認為與普京執行廉能政府政策有關。蘇爾科夫負責管理政府轄下的斯科爾科沃創業基金會，今年4月基金會副總裁別利秋科夫遭指控違規使用資金。（圖片來源：http://state.kremlin.ru/administration/7495）

普京身邊有一位草根出身但發
跡於銀行界的重要智囊就是蘇爾柯
夫。蘇爾柯夫（Владисла́в Ю́рьевич
Сурко́в）是長年擔任普京辦公室的
副主任，梅德維傑夫執政時期此人
進入政府擔任副總理，仍然繼續跟
隨普京身邊，蘇爾柯夫是車臣族
裔。他是「納什」的青年運動的是
主要贊助者。「納什」青年運動組
織成立於2005年，創辦人是Василий
Григорьевич Якеме́нко，雅凱緬科，
是「我們一起走」與「納什」青年

◆ 雅凱緬科，「納什」青年運
動的創辦人，俄羅斯聯邦政
府青年事務署的領導人。
（圖片來源：http://premier.
gov.ru/events/news/12923/
photolents.html）

運動的創辦人，2008年成為俄羅斯聯邦政府青年事務署的領導
人。成為青年從事社會運動而從政的代表人物。他是支持普京
政策的青年黨團的領袖人物。

　　年輕人所處的轉型時代，面對的是學校教材混亂，獎學
金減少與學費提高影響學生就學權益的各種問題。青年是國家
的人才來源，普京執政之後立刻將資金投入到教育和青年事務
當中。儘管普京要培養年輕人的選票，但這應該只是發展青年
計畫的一個附帶成果，更加急迫性的問題不如說如何正確引導
俄羅斯青年積極參與國家青年政策的制定以及落實青年關心切
身利益問題的長期發展戰略目標更為貼切，國家如何把提升國
力之後的經濟資源一部份用在青年人的成長需求上是至關重
要的。年輕人對於自身利益關切的訴求被普京適時地接受，
他們對國家民族產生的熱情與信心剛好是普京強國政策的基

礎，他們將來會代表國家站在國際舞台上與參與俄羅斯的改革，這是後來俄羅斯青年團體「納什」有發展與生存空間的社會基礎。

　　事實上，普京的青年政策主要為他們組織各類活動提供經費贊助，以及長期補助組織成員申請莫斯科大學與獎助學金建立獎勵機制，這些正面因素對年輕人具有激勵作用。普京支持了年輕人的政治訴求，所以成為了年輕人崇拜的偶像，但如果理解普京主觀上去發展青年團體作為執政選票，就顛倒了這種發展關係，試圖把俄羅斯年輕人對普京的欣賞解讀為一種盲目的崇拜或是被普京操控的極端團體，這都將會使持有這種思想的人陷入一種疑惑：為何「納什」的青年領袖會經常與俄羅斯獨立媒體人在一起？或是他們如何能公開與常態性地參加電視臺談話性節目以及進行社會公益活動？如果這些年輕人只是一群沒有思想理念的盲目極端份子崇拜者？

　　「納什」青年成員的夏令營活動與社會活動經費來源於都是由大企業捐贈，成員也可以到這些企業實習和工作，經濟因素激勵的青年人的參與動機，國家命運的使命感與價值觀凝聚了他們的愛國共識，在媒體輿論上他們與西方支持的反對派組織的遊行形成相互制衡的一股力量，畢竟前蘇聯國家在西方政府支持下發生了推翻執政者的顏色革命，俄羅斯人不希望俄羅斯政權是由西方的政治干預來主導，如果只有一種西方意識型態聲音佔據俄羅斯媒體輿論的版面，那麼民眾對於自身生活不滿的情緒將會和這些外部批普京政策的聲音結合成一股反普京政府的力量，果真如此的話，那麼內部的民族分裂與政治鬥爭必然只有加劇，這種內外結合的輿論上力量必將打擊

俄羅斯再次崛起？──雙頭鷹的亞太政策與戰略思想

◆ 普京與「納什」青年團員見面。
（圖片來源：http://bsx.ru/~gong/lj/grab/putin/92903265_2.jpg）

到普京的強國良好願意：俄羅斯內部改善生活條件以及外部
參與全球治理的目標。而支持普京的青年黨運動可以適當扮演
平衡外部輿論的壓力，俄羅斯本國媒體的輿論將會被來自內部
兩股強烈的意識形態鬥爭所佔據，普京的強國政策在幕後至少
受到一定程度的保護，普京自身不需要正面與俄羅斯獨立媒
體為敵。

　　俄羅斯《生意人報》記者奧列格・卡申（Олег Владимирович
Кашин）2010年11月6日在莫斯科遭兩名男子襲擊。按照美聯社
的說法，俄公路建設行業腐敗嚴重，牽涉不少官員。關於築路
專案的報導可能威脅開發商等多方利益。俄記者還聯名上書總
統表示「政府應該為國內媒體工作者的安全負直接責任」。

　　卡申被毆導重傷住院引起了國際社會的關注，身為一名
獨立記者，對於俄羅斯記者所處的社會感到恐懼與不滿。卡申
與多數俄羅斯記者都強調了記者被打或被殺是突顯俄羅斯新聞
自由面臨的惡劣環境。俄羅斯獨立記者的威脅來自於社會存在
某種極端情緒和流氓混混文化的混合體，這些人不應該與有組

◆ 民眾於內務部前手持標語並要求找出毆
打卡申記者的幕後指使者，允予嚴厲懲
罰。（圖片來源：http://www.flickr.com/
photos/yuri_timofeyev/5154106397/）

織青年運動混淆在一起，因為獨立記者的批判言論和知名度很
容易成為這些街頭小流氓或是極端情緒狂熱者的攻擊目標，這
類極端份子的特點就是有意或是無意地對俄羅斯政府持不同意
見的名人作為洩憤的目標，因為他們從媒體上認出這些不同意
見者而簡單理解為反俄羅斯民族者，這種現象存在於蘇聯解體
之後。俄羅斯記者的個人生命安全問題是蘇聯解體之後俄羅斯
普遍社會安全問題的最集中表現。

　　卡申被毆在俄羅斯高層形成兩個直接影響：其一是政府
輿論政策多元化的回歸，擺脫絕對的愛國主義觀作為執政的核
心基礎，進入另一個國家社會正常化的提升階段；再者就是社
會治安的改善，把國家安全問題從民族分離的概念上轉為現實
社會不安分子的監管，獨立記者的被毆事件還是突顯了社會安
全與治安的根本問題。普京既然已經執政了，未來輿論的導向

◆ 梅德維傑夫總統於2011年11月18日會
見卡申 。（圖片來源：http://kremlin.
ru/photo/1411）

應該從現在的愛國主義回歸到一種多元思想與民族和諧的包容
態度上，唯有如此不同的意見才能適時地參與政府決策的過程
並且發揮一種意見平衡的調整作用。卡申被毆事件之所以驚動
普京和梅德維傑夫表態，是俄羅斯長期以來獨立記者生命安全
受到威脅以及生存空間被壓縮的一種整體表現，而國家領導者
對於記者因為批判政府意見而受到人身攻擊的安全問題負有責
任。國家領導者首先應該發表言論，表示獨立記者的存在對於
俄羅斯民主發展與言論自由具有絕對的貢獻，這樣許多極端份
子與社會混混之流的人也會受到這種正面言論的影響，不會輕
易把這些名人當作攻擊的對象，以減少持不同政見者在社會上
遭到歧視和受到攻擊的可能性，政府要將保護記者的生命財產
安全當作社會治安狀況的首要指標；其次，才會是這些獨立記
者的言論對普京政府所產生的威脅，事實上這種威脅在民眾對

普京的信任和支持下作用不大。相反地，俄羅斯獨立記者的批判貢獻遠遠超過他們對於政府執政所產生的威脅，這是俄羅斯會的一股刺激力量，普京深深體會與了解這點的重要性，這都有利於普京2012年重返克里姆林宮執政後以及未來與反對勢力建立互動與溝通的管道。

上海合作組織的能源整合趨勢

——俄羅斯能源戰略思想與意涵

◆ 照片取自俄羅斯總統府／2012-06-06，北京：普京上任總統後出訪中國參加上海合作組織高峰會，與當時習近平副主席見面，普京表示了很高興他們之間的個人友誼和工作接觸能夠繼續延續，同時也強調了俄羅斯和中國的合作不僅在於經濟的領域，還要關注維護國際安全和世界經濟秩序的穩定。

能源在上海合作組織架構下是最有前景的合作項目。然而目前要如何將上海合作組織的機制從地緣政治的特點轉向優先發展經濟、能源與科技一體化的整合方向上來。對於中國方面而言，俄羅斯供應中國能源所獲得的利益可以解決俄羅斯社會福利發展所需要的資金，而俄羅斯方面認為，能源的供應影響了亞太地區的安全與平衡，如果中俄之間的互信沒有達到一定的穩定程度，在上合組織架構下的整合仍有很大的困難。當然過去中蘇之間在1969年珍寶島[1]的軍事衝突使得俄羅斯對於

---

[1] 珍寶島在1991年已經正式劃入中國的領土，對俄羅斯而言，這是一場雙輸且沒有必要發生的戰爭，因為1969年，中國軍隊試圖登島的行為完全會引起俄方的嚴厲打擊，俄羅斯在這方面完全是強硬的態度，俄國的邊防軍有絕對的權力對侵入領土的敵人開火，儘管該島完全位在中國的河道領域內並且歷史上烏蘇里江是中國固有的領土，但是根據中俄在十九世紀中葉以後所簽訂的雙邊條約，俄方認定邊界是在河靠近中國河岸的這邊，顯然中俄雙方在簽訂時認定與解讀就有問題，如果中國不通過談判而直接登島的話，這完全無庸置疑的會引起俄方的直接打擊。這樣的軍事衝突只會將兩

中國缺乏信任，而五十年代末開使醞釀中蘇之間的意識形態爭論使得中國心理對俄羅斯產生憎恨，儘管在中蘇關係惡化以前，中國有將近半個世紀的發展是仰賴俄羅斯軍事的支持。

　　換言之，上海合作組織要從一個軍事政治合作的機制轉型成為經濟能源的機制還面臨了誰是這個機制的主導者──俄羅斯？中國？如果中國在亞太地區的關係趨於緊張，俄羅斯就是唯一可以支持中國的國家了：能源供應和武器輸出。那麼，俄羅斯與中國的過度合作是否有好處呢？歷史表明，俄羅斯會小心謹慎處理中俄關係：速度不會太過、也不能太慢。俄羅斯發展亞太地區的國家間關係，與美國亞洲再平衡政策一樣，都必須考量國內經濟發展的需求，以俄羅斯目前已經是世貿成員來看，俄羅斯的亞洲政策會更加靈活而不受中國的牽制，中國在處理東海與南海問題時面臨與美國的衝突，此時俄羅斯的能源政策在上合組織中的作用對中國來說是至關重要的。

◆ http://mail.inoforum.ru/forum/…

◆ http://www.vlms.ru/foto36.html

國的信任完全擊潰，之後正常化的過程會是漫長和持久的行為。犧牲的代價太大。包括中共會犧牲台灣的利益或是中俄的利益來解決黨內鬥爭和與美國之間的妥協等等。這完全表明中共的處境和困境，挑戰依然很大。

一、俄羅斯能源戰略思想特點

　　俄羅斯能源戰略的制定，主要是用來確認國家能源發展的中長期目標與制定執行的具體任務。2003年，俄羅斯政府出台了第一份有關俄羅斯能源發展的戰略報告，自此確認了能源戰略作為國家發展內外政策最重要的執行方針。俄羅斯能源部直屬的能源戰略研究所，自2006年開始積極研擬相關政策，目前俄羅斯的能源戰略是制定到2030年：《俄羅斯能源戰略概念現階段到2030年》（Концепция Энергетической стратегии России на период до 2030 года），這份文件已經在2009年11月13日經由俄羅斯政府批准生效執行了。

這份能源發展戰略計畫書的基本方針如下：

第一、落實現階段到2020年能源發展任務與目標。

第二、評估國家社會經濟發展趨勢以及掌握經濟與能源互動關係。

第三、掌握俄羅斯能源需求前景。

第四、了解能源政策基本條件和其重要組成要素。

第五、俄羅斯燃料－能源總體儲藏量的前景。

第六、評估2030年能源戰略執行預期結果和落實體系。

第七、建構區域內部能源直接運輸管道的可行性，鼓勵投資與降低中國中東與非洲石油遭受阻斷的風險。

第八、平衡上海合作組織架構下能源出口與進口的關係，充分
　　　考慮雙邊國家關係和平等權利。

第九、世界能源儲藏量大量集中在上合組織的國家當中，25%
　　　石油儲藏量，50%天然氣，50%鈾，35%媒，中印都是能
　　　源需求增長的國家，目前也是上合組織積極的參與者。

第十、確保上合組織的合作關係以及減少對俄羅斯和中國的敵
　　　對因素也是至關重要的，區域的安全與穩定有利於中亞
　　　國家石油輸往全世界的能源市場，同時也是上合組織存
　　　在的價值和作用。

第十一、將上合組織轉型成為全球的能源體系，應是上合組織
　　　　成員國希望看到的發展遠景。中俄之間對於能源價格
　　　　和能源合作的態度仍存在歧見，這是使上海合作組織
　　　　轉型為經濟合作機制發展緩慢的主要因素。

　　目前上合組織成員之間的能源關係主要是雙邊關係，例
如已經存在的石油運輸項目工程包括：裡海石油管道集團公
司（Каспийский трубопроводный консорциум），阿塔蘇－阿拉
上科伊石油管道（нефтепроводы Атасу-Алашанькоу），《東西
伯利亞－太平洋》中國分支管道（《Восточная Сибирь-Тихий
океан》）；土庫曼－烏茲別克斯坦－哈薩克－中國天然氣管
道（газопроводы Туркмения-Узбекистан-Казахстан-Китай），正
在修建當中的雅庫奇雅－哈巴羅夫斯克－符拉迪沃斯克的俄羅
斯通往中國的天然氣管道（проектируемый газопровод Якутия-
Хабаровск-Владивосток с возможным отводом в Китай 2016 г.），
這條管道工程預計在2016年完工。上述這些能源管道彼此還存

在一定程度的競爭和排擠效應，因為過去中國採取兩手策略同時與中亞和俄羅斯建立能源合作計畫，現在如果上合組織成員國希望整合內部資源，如何整合到上海合作組織的架構下關係到俄羅斯對能源市場的整體控制。前蘇聯加盟共和國的獨聯體中亞成員國家基本上與俄羅斯完成了軍事和經濟的整合，中亞的經濟成長與國防安全基本上完全仰賴俄羅斯。這樣是否意味著未來上合組織由俄羅斯擔任領導者，但是中國是能源上合組織中最大的消費國與進口國，中國是否會受到石油輸出國家的操控也是影響中國整合意願的重要因素。

黑龍江省社科院東北亞所研究員宋魁指出，對俄聯邦東西伯利亞和遠東輸油系統發展作出以下規定：東西伯利亞方向：保障在東西伯利亞和薩哈共和國（雅庫特）形成新的石油開採中心，包括建設「尤魯布琴－托霍莫油田－阿欽斯克－安加爾斯克」石油管道和「塔拉坎油田和上瓊油田－安加爾斯克」石油管道。俄羅斯要進入亞太能源市場，就必須建設「安加爾斯克－納霍德卡」（後調整為泰納線）石油管道（年輸油能力為5000萬噸）及其通往中國大慶的分支管道（年輸油能力為3000萬噸）。遠東方向：建立從薩哈林大陸架進入亞太市場和南亞的油氣管道，「薩哈林—1」項目包括鋪設年輸油能力為1250萬噸石油的管道，它從海上經過韃靼海峽抵達德卡斯特里油港（哈巴羅夫斯克邊疆區）。「薩哈林—2」專案的一期工程需要建設兩條長800公里的陸地管道，以便將石油和天然氣從薩哈林島北部輸送到南部。為實現遠東方向的管道建設計畫，還需要建設新油港和擴大現有油港。

二、上合組織中存在的整合障礙

2005年12月在烏茲別克斯坦首都塔什干召開的「中亞能源市場：趨勢和前景」。2006年6月，俄聯邦總統普京在上海合作組織國家元首上海峰會上十分明確地把其視為已經具有實用性的一項倡議。普京說：我認為這是最急迫的議題，首要解決的問題就是運輸和傳播。

目前在上海合作組織中客觀上存在阻撓擴大經濟整合範圍的具體的障礙包括：

第一、上海合作組織內缺乏一套共同的社會經濟發展戰略，當然這與成員國之間國家利益的區隔和意見紛歧有關。

第二、成員國之間經濟發展潛力的不均等，俄羅斯和中亞國家擔心來自於中國財政與投資能力的經濟控制與貿易威脅。

第三、積極發展整合項目，包括海關同盟和歐亞經濟一體化空間，缺乏中國的參與，唯有參與其中方能解決架構內的問題與維護上海合作組織的能源經濟圈的利益。

俄羅斯方面將「能源俱樂部」視為上合組織構架下解決能源問題的協調和分析中心。但是機制必須要結構清楚而不是封閉式的機構，為此可與上合組織之外的國家、國際組織或是商業機構進行直接的互動。

烏茲別克斯坦政治研究中心主任認為：近幾年，世界市場形勢顯示，能源開採、勘探和運輸方面的問題越來越迫切，建立新的發電設備的趨勢也越來越明顯。首先是，南亞和東南亞碳氫化合物的消費量空前增長；其次是，北美和歐洲碳氫化合物的消費水準持續走高；再次是，一些原料傳統開採地區的資源正在逐漸枯竭。全球電力生產和消費市場的形勢都在增長。能源消費國正在尋求對問題的各種解決方案：從積極投資開發國外有前景的專案，到對能源生產國施加直接外交壓力和強制壓力。因此，盛產油氣和鈾的上海合作組織成員國和觀察員國的重要性日益增長。這使該組織唯一能在「生產國和消費國」之間建立一個能大大影響全球能源市場的平衡機構。這些問題涉及能源勘探、開採、運輸和電力生產的相互配合。

三、「能源俱樂部」面臨的問題

第一、促進能源政策的和諧並且推動組織成員國和其他觀察國
　　　　或是合作夥伴之間的長期能源發展計畫。
第二、制訂與研議具體執行能源安全政策的措施。
第三、發展上海合作組織架構下共同的能源傳播運輸系統。
第四、創建共同的經濟機制落實成員國家的能源政策。
第五、協調成員國家的能源投資計畫。
第六、提高信息化的合作。
第七、推動一致的能源行動走向世界能源的市場。

關於電力的部分，整合的重要部分還有將吉爾吉斯坦、塔吉克斯坦和烏茲別克斯坦的水電競爭衝突轉為向帕米爾地區的印度和中國輸出，優化俄羅斯、哈薩克斯坦與中國之間的發電容量。避免俄羅斯和其他中亞國家包括烏茲別克斯坦、哈薩克斯坦與土庫曼對於中國能源市場的激烈競爭。聯合開發天然氣加工和天然氣化工產品。要考慮印度和中國的利益和共同的煉油廠現代化問題，要協調俄羅斯和中亞國家能源的出口政策。

　　劉朝鋒與劉曉玲在「新時期上海合作組織能源合作探析」一文中指出：在上海合作組織內，中國、俄羅斯、哈薩克斯坦是主要的能源生產、消費和出口國，因此三國在上海合作組織框架內進行能源合作的過程中，起著主導性的作用。近年來，中俄關係不斷發展。自1996年4月雙方決定建立戰略協作夥伴關係後，兩國元首於2001年7月簽署了《中俄睦鄰友好合作條約》，為保障兩國關係穩定發展奠定了牢固的法律基礎。2005年6月2日中俄兩國簽訂了《關於中俄國界東段的補充協定》，徹底解決了困擾兩國關係的邊界問題，為雙邊關係的進一步發展掃清了障礙。中哈自建交以來，雙邊關係全面發展。早在1997年兩國政府就簽訂了油氣合作協議，2005年兩國元首決定將雙邊關係提升為戰略夥伴關係。哈俄兩國同為獨聯體成員國，兩國有著傳統的戰略友好關係，互把對方視為外交的優先方向。這種良好的三邊政治關係，是順利開展能源合作的基礎和保證。而上海合作組織五週年紀念峰會的成功舉行和《上海合作組織五週年宣言》的發表，更為各成員國深化包括能源合作在內的經濟合作注入了新的動力。

深化能源－體化進程

　　能源政策的整合應該要追隨共同歐亞一體化的主要目標，正因如此才有可能使區域組織的社會空間轉變成為新的形式，從一個技術的提供者變成為科技智慧的領先者。要成為科技的領導者必須要有創新科技的機制，全面將能源的網絡和效能現代化，提升改善研發條件、提升科研人員的研發創新能力和支持基礎的科研工作。整合的部分要包含能源運輸的基礎設施部分以及提升創新開發油田項目的技術水準和經濟效益，建立進入電力和能源市場的互動條件。

　　總體而言，能源合作與相互整合是目前上海合作組織進行經濟一體化最急迫解決和實踐的問題，其中要清除能源發展的相互衝突並且協調共同的能源政策，要把上合組織全球能源的發展政策提上議事日程，取代根據自己單一的政策，為有如此上合組織才能有效參與世界能源的競爭市場，與歐盟和美國並駕齊驅。避免俄羅斯和中國在區域內的長期對抗，包括在能源領域當中的分歧，有效整合上合組織內中亞成員國家和俄羅斯的有效合作。

參考文獻

1. А.И. Громов, Энергетическое измерение развития ШОС. 26 ноября 2012 г. Финансовый Университет при Правительстве РФ, Москва.

2. 俄羅斯能源戰略研究所官網：http://www.energystrategy.ru

3. 俄新網，http://en.rian.ru/world/20060615/49512082.html

4. 卡里莫娃：《俄羅斯中亞東歐市場》2007年第5期。

5. 宋魁，俄羅斯國家能源戰略剖析，2011，作者個人官網。 http://www.china5e.com/blog/?uid-3867-action-viewspace-itemid-748

6. 劉朝鋒與劉曉玲，在「新時期上海合作組織能源合作探析」，西伯利亞研究2007年2期。

Russia and China Relations:

Security and Integration

Hu, Feng-Yung

Yuan Ze University & National Taiwan University

The Collective Security conception has been deepened in the Cold War period when the world was divided into two parts and bipolar military confrontation was formed. However, after the collapse of USSR, the Cold War ended and the geopolitical sphere has changed a lot with the whole crisis in Russia. Russia started to consolidate the Central Asian region as her most important Eurasian foreign policy after the liberalization and democratization process in the post-communism era and improve the relationship with China in the second ruling period of Yeltsin. Russia's Asian-pacific strategy is almost formed after Putin returned to the Kremlin but SCO plays an important role of establishing the mutual trust and communication between Russia and China in the past decade. After the global financial crisis and US's withdraw from Iraq and Afghanistan, it seems to be that SCO plays the more and more important role not only in regional security for anti-terrorism and drug criminals, but also in energy trade. The author attempts to analyze SCO from Russia's political and strategic thinking to see the China's challenges and US' Factors in balancing the Sino-Russian relationship. This study examined the Russian attitudes toward the SCO and China's possible responses to them.

Keywords: SCO, collective security, geopolitics, energy security strategy

Regional Relations between Russia and China

When it says on the historically remained disputes on borders between Russia and China, it reminds the bilateral people of the existing problems of national security and national interests. For meeting the demands of the rising powers, these two countries need to cooperate with each other economically and strategically. Obviously, China and Russia play more and more important roles in the Asian-Pacific region where the United States is implementing the rebalancing policy under the Obama administration. In the end of the Cold War, the normalization process was realized by the negotiations between Gorbachev and Deng Xiaoping after the ideological fighting and boundary military conflicts in 60's and 70's. The state level relations were more important than the regional interaction. Since the Soviet Union's disintegration in the early 1990s, the two countries have for the most part acted on the basis of shared interests-particularly in maintaining stability in Central Asia, whose energy supplies are vital for both countries' economic development (Weitz 2012: 72).

After Putin took the presidency in 2000, to resume the former control in Central Asia and to balance the westernized foreign policy toward the East has been the priority for the Russian Federation. With the strengthened potential influence of the Asian-Pacific countries on the world, how to accelerate the function of the neighboring regions between Russian Far East (RFE) and Chinese North East (CNE) has been put on the agenda especially after the 2008 global financial crisis. After Putin came back again to the Kremlin in 2012, the tendency of Russia to consolidate the integration in the Central Asian region and broaden the influential sphere in the Asian-Pacific region will complicate the Russia-China future relations. Therefore, the future perspective relations between Russia and China deserve to be explored prudentially.

Russia is a trans-regional great power with some vital national interests in many regions. In addition, Russia is China's biggest neighbor state. Thus, in terms of region, some strategic overlap cannot be avoided between Russia and China. Among of these strategic overlap regions, at least three regions are much closed linked with China's national security. The first strategic overlap region is Northeast Asia. Some complex and sensitive international issues are sparkled in this region, such as the North Korean issue, The Sino-Korean-Japanese historical issue, a serial of disputed territory issues and so on. The second strategic overlap region is Central Asia, including Kazakhstan, Kyrgyzstan, Tajikistan, Turkmenistan, and Uzbekistan. Strategic overlap regions between Russia and China are also impacting China's political security. (Chen Ou 2011: 82-84).

Traditionally, China relies on Russia to dissolve the international isolation, and this ideological, physiological and geographical intimate relationship easily makes China seek for help from Russia. Nowadays, Russia's attitude toward China in terms of selling weapons and resources deeply influences the balance and stability in Asia. From time to time, China regards the Sino-Russian relations as the cornerstone of the maintaining stability and security in Asia. In other words, framing the strategic and constructive partnership between Russia and China is the protective umbrella for China to face the pressure from the United States concerning of the territorial disputes in Taiwan straits, East Sea and Southern China Sea. Undoubtedly, Russia in some kind of degree plays the supporting and crucial role for China in face of the American containment in the Asian-Pacific region. The islands disputes between Japan and China in East Sea also irritate China to rise its military proliferation. With little in the way of domestic production of fuel, raw materials, or timber, Japan is more dependent than other major industrial nations on imports of these commodities. The rising energy and raw material prices turned Japan's near-complete dependence on imports of these products into a source of painful costs (Rawski 2012:419).

The Central Asia suffered terrorism and corruption which led to the color revolution to overthrow the ruling government. The former president of Kyrgyz Akaev was overthrown and fled to Russia, now working as the professor at Moscow State University. He has his political philosophy about the small country implementing his foreign policy among the great powers and that is serving a place where they would be able to cooperate and coordinate their interests. He said: "I have in mind the national conception and we have applied it to our relations with Russia in the first place. Relationships with Russia are high on the list of our country's foreign policy priorities - for me that is very important. Now I would like to dwell on the subject of multi-vectorial diplomacy by which I mean the relationships between my country and the great power triangle: Russia, the US and China. I shall not go here into details of twenty-two centuries of our relations with China. At all times the trends were positive: China is our good neighbor and friend. American and Russian bases on our territory appeared precisely as a result of this approach. They serve global and regional security as well as national security of Kyrgyzstan and Russia. This is very important at the time when the leaders of international terrorism remain resolved to attack our countries. We should also bear in mind that the seat of international terrorism in Afghanistan is still smoldering and poisons the atmosphere all over the world."(Akaev 2004:90-92)

China is well ahead of Russia and India as to the degree of its engagement in the global economy, including the realm of trade and investment flows. Thus, it understandably desires to play the role as the engine of the Asian economy, as well as becoming an "active growth factor" in the global economy on the whole. At the same time, however, China may experience problems in the future as it tries to consolidate positions in global economic relations. It has vulnerable areas, like a scanty resource base, together with a lack of affiliation with any integration-minded regional groups. Thus, one may expect to see a marked increase in China's efforts to eliminate or minimize those problems (Vladimir Portyakov: 139).

Since the Shanghai Cooperation Organization (SCO) was founded in 2001, the SCO has essentially functioned as a Chinese-Russian condominium, providing Beijing and Moscow with a convenient multilateral framework to manage their interests in Central Asia. The bilateral defense relationship has evolved in recent years to become more institutionalized and better integrated. Nevertheless, the two governments also remain suspicious about each other's activities in Central Asia, where their state-controlled firms compete for energy resources. Russia plans to continue transforming the Collective Security Treaty Organization (CSTO), which excludes China, into Central Asia's primary multilateral security institution. Russian plans to create an EU-like arrangement among the former Soviet republics could irritate Beijing because such a development could impede China's economic access to Central Asia (Weitz 2012: 72-7).

Despite the fact that Russia and China have contradictions, the SCO and their energy monopoly has unrest the balance in Asia.

Obviously, China's rising has changed the traditional balance in Asia After the Second World War and this has aroused the suspicion and difficulty to integrate with other countries. To reduce the economic dependence on China has become the common thinking for many countries and this will challenge China' economical growth in the future.

At the regional level, the development of economic and other ties between the contiguous Russian Far East (RFE) and Chinese North East (CNE) has lagged behind breakthroughs at the national level. Improving state level relations have been complicated by fluctuations in interregional relations. Economic cooperation and regional development are more prominent, and Chinese migration and associated problems much less prominent (Sullivan & Renz 2010:262).

Economy issue of the trade and investment is the central concern in both countries' media coverage. In either Chinese national or regional media coverage, the first frame emphasizes a combination of Russian natural resources and land and Chinese expertise, labour, goods and capital. The predominant frame in both Russian national and regional newspapers is the idea that economic cooperation between Russia and China is a necessity for the development of the country's economy (Sullivan & Renz 2010:277-8).

The second level salient issue is the law and order which represents the unofficial economy. The Russian national media emphasizes increasing law-enforcement cooperation between China and Russia, particularly regarding international organized crime and terrorism, whilst discussing illegal migration into Russia as a serious problem for the country generally. In the contrast, China part stresses the hard-working of the Chinese workers in RFE (Sullivan & Renz 2010:279).

The third level issue is the regional issue. Both sides emphasize that the regional cooperation in the contiguous RFE and CNE is beneficial for both countries because it plays the engine of the economic growth in both countries (Sullivan & Renz 2010:280). The forth concerned level is about the state interaction. China media paid more attention to the traditional friendship, which is based on increasing military cooperation and the final demarcation of the Eastern boarder. Russian media paid more attention to the Military cooperation and confidence-building measures than the border demarcation and territory concession (Sullivan & Renz 2010:281).

Therefore, it seems to be that Russia regards the mutual trust and cooperation mechanism building as the preconditions of weapons and national resources selling, however, China more focuses on the concrete benefits which could be obtained by money. (Sullivan & Renz 2010:282) concluded that the treatment of RFE – CNE relations as a priority area in the strategic partnership between the two countries is encouraging. However, whether the document will serve to level regional expectations about cooperation and substantially improve the potential for regionalism in the RFE – CNE in the long term remains to be seen.

The Meaning of Collective Security of SCO

International security cooperation usually takes one of two forms. A classical collective security organization is designed to promote international security through regulating the behavior of its member states. A defensive security organization is designed to protect a group of states from threats emanating from a challenging state or group of states. Both forms of security cooperation bind states to act in concert with respect to threats presented by other states. The emergence of non-state actors such as terrorist or extremist organizations challenges traditional forms of collective security. Threats from political extremism, terrorism, and outlaw organizations have grown in visibility during the past decade in the countries of Eurasia.[1] (Gregory Gleason & Marat E. Shaihutdino, 2005)

In this climate of a shared sense of common threat from non-state actors Fand on the background of perceived encroachment from the sole remaining Superpower, the United States, the Eurasian countries returned to the bargaining table. In these circumstances a number of security organization already in nascent form, the Shanghai Cooperation Organization (SCO), the Conference on Interaction and Confidence Building Measures, and the CIS Collective Security Treaty Organization (CSTO), were rapidly expanded and further institutionalized to address the new security challenges.[2] (Gregory Gleason & Marat E. Shaihutdino,

---

[1] Gregory Gleason & Marat E. Shaihutdino(2005), " Collective Security and Non-State Actors in Eurasia." International Studies Perspectives (2005) 6: 274.

Eurasia is also sometimes used in geopolitics to refer to organizations of or affairs concerning the post-Soviet states, in particular Russia, the Central Asian republics, and the Transcaucasian republics.

A prominent example of this usage is in the name of the Eurasian Economic Community, the organization including Kazakhstan, Russia, and some of their neighbors, and headquartered in Moscow and Astana. The word "Eurasia" is often used in Kazakhstan as the name of the continent or region in which that country is located.

Now the Russian policy-makers have adjusted the foreign policy to the Eastern and southern Asia. Therefore, Putin's administration prefers to use the conception of Asian-pacific instead of Eurasia. It symbolizes that Russia's foreign policy is tuning his angle from Europe and Central Asia to Asian-Pacific region. The integration with the Central Asia is finished after the global financial crisis. Russian energy market is shriveling and needs to open up the Asian market.

[2] Gregory Gleason & Marat E. Shaihutdino(2005) Collective Security and Non-State Actors in Eurasia, International Studies Perspectives (2005) 6: 276.

2005) After the collapse of USSR, Russia lost the protection of collective security system of Warsaw Treaty Organization and how to establish the new unions with the former Soviet Union States became the imperative missions in the first decade of post-communism era.

By accounting for the deleterious effects of globalization (non-state actors) on world security, Huntington also contributes to our knowledge by updating realism. The title of the book, after all, does not just consist of The Clash of Civilizations, but the Clash of Civilizations and the Remaking of World Order. Global politics is increasingly replicating the patterns of diversity and plurality found in domestic politics, with "one crucial difference." It is all a question of shifting from the chaotic realm of sub-state actors to state actors, moving away from the anarchic state of affairs left by the collapse of Communism. Interestingly enough, one of the best illustrations of how this arrangement would work can be seen in his handling of the Muslim world. This includes protection for their values.[3] (Emad El-Din Aysha, 2003) Globalization is the vast conception and force which make the world more interactive and dependent. One of the concerned issues is the cultural or civilization conflicts which could damage the traditional ethics and moral principles in a certain community with strong religion.

After the collapse of USSR, the passive impression exists both in Russia and China around the ideological difference, boundary disputes and illegal trade. Therefore, Yeltsin and Jiang Zeming were anxious to repair bilateral relationships. The "Shanghai Five" cooperative

---

[3] Emad El-Din Aysha(2003) Samuel Huntington and the Geopolitics of American Identity: The Function of Foreign Policy in America's Domestic Clash of Civilizations, International Studies Perspectives (2003) 4:128.

mechanism occurred in this distrust and unfriendly atmosphere which began from the ideology debate between Mao and Khrushchev. However, these two countries' leaders Yeltsin and Jiang Zeming have good personal friendship and this helped improve bilateral relationship and consolidate Central Asian region which suffers economic and terror crisis. Despite Russia and China historically has the boundary disputes, Chinese philosophy had great influence on Russia' writers and philosophers in 18-19th centuries and Russia did have influenced on Chinese intelligentsia in 19-20th centuries. The cultural interaction can improve the relationships between these two giant countries with ancient civilizations. From 2007 with the promotion of Russia's Russkiy Mir and China's Confucius Institute, these two countries started to hold Russian National Year in China and Chinese National Year in Russia and under this cooperation framework the governmental departments and media enterprises from both counties stated to conduct. The "cultural cooperation and exchange" might avoid cultural conflicts and colonization.

Ideological differences and military confrontations in Soviet time reduced bilateral trade and increased the defense budget. Due to the boundary demarcation and disarmament, Russia and China intend to establish a long-term negotiating mechanism and SCO was established initially for resolving these disputes, then gradually developing toward active cooperation in many areas such as conducting military operations for anti-terrorism, improving trade and economic relationships to achieve bilateral trade amount up to the symbolic index. Therefore, SCO is anticipated to be based on establishing the mutual trust among these countries. With the Putin's Asian-Pacific strategy and China's new leadership, SCO will play the more and more crucial role in controlling world energy supply and international military intervention to increase their power in global governance such as in UN Security Council. It shows that after the global financial crisis the western countries need to take Russia' and China's opinions into consideration and the relationship between Russia and China in SCO has aroused more and more attention from the outside world.

The Short History and Organizational Framework of SCO

The SCO, initially a "constructive partnership" in 1994, which was based on the bilateral Sino-Russian security cooperative arrangement and gradually developed into a multilateral framework for strategic partnerships., was upgraded to a strategic partnership in 1996, when the "Shanghai Five" was founded (with Kazakhstan, Kyrgyzstan, and Tajikistan). These states (and Uzbekistan, which became a member in 2001) together with China and Russia allied together to establish the SCO which was designed to address the issues of terrorism, separatism, and extremism. Mongolia (2004), India, Iran, Pakistan (2005) and Afghanistan (2012) are the observer states. Belarus, Sri Lanka and Turkey (2012) are the dialogue partners.

SCO's predecessor, the "Shanghai Five" mechanism, originated and grew from the endeavor by China, Russia, Kazakhstan, Kyrgyzstan and Tajikistan to strengthen confidence-building and disarmament in the border regions. In 1996 and 1997, their heads of state met in Shanghai and Moscow respectively and signed *the Treaty on Deepening Military Trust in Border Regions* in Shanghai and *the Treaty on Reduction of Military Forces in Border Regions* in Moscow. The topics of the meeting gradually extended from building up trust in the border regions to mutually beneficial cooperation in the political, security, diplomatic, economic, trade and other areas among the five states. Subsequent annual summits of the Shanghai Five group occurred in Almaty (Kazakhstan) in 1998, in Bishkek (Kyrgyzstan) in 1999, and in Dushanbe (Tajikistan) in 2000.

On the fifth anniversary of the Shanghai Five in June 2001, the heads of states met in Shanghai and signed a joint declaration admitting Uzbekistan as member of the Shanghai Five mechanism and then jointly issued the Declaration on the Establishment of the Shanghai Cooperation Organization. The document announced that for the purpose of upgrading the level of cooperation to more effectively seize opportunities and deal with new challenges and threats. In June 2002, the heads of SCO member states met in St. Petersburg and signed the SCO Charter, which clearly expounded the SCO purposes and principles, organizational structure, form of operation, cooperation, orientation and external relations, marking the actual establishment of this new organization in the sense of international law.[4]

The structure of SCO is the framework of functioning which could be divided into three parts: intergovernmental mechanism of annual summits of states heads, governments heads (Prime Ministers), meetings of heads of ministries or departments; permanent organs of Secretariat and Regional Counter-Terrorism Structures; nongovernmental institutions: SCO Business Council, SCO Interbank Consortiums and SCO Forums. The SCO Organizational Structure Chart could be illustrated as following:

---

[4] Shanghai Cooperation Organization (SCO), http://www. globalsecurity.org/military/world/int/sco.htm

Table 1: The Structure of SCO[5]

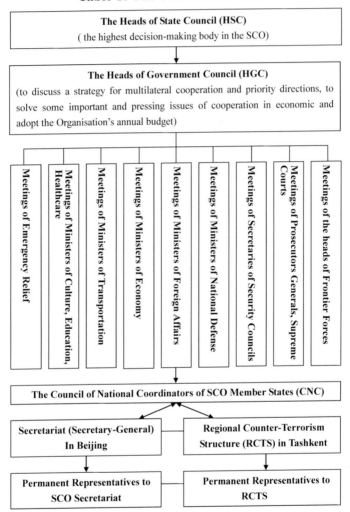

---

[5] http://www.sco-ec.gov.cn/crweb/scor/info/Article.jsp?col_no=321&a_no=56546
http://www.sco-ec.gov.cn/crweb/scor/info/Article.jsp?col_no=321&a_no=56545
http://en.wikipedia.org/wiki/Shanghai_Cooperation_Organisation
http://www.sectsco.org/EN/brief.asp

From the SCO documents, we can know that the SCO time by time is becoming a more functional and effective intergovernmental organization. However, the SCO is influenced by the international situation and Sino-Russian relations. At the June 16-17, 2004 SCO summit, held in Tashkent, Uzbekistan and the staff of the Executive Committee of the Regional Counter-Terrorism Structure (RCTS) is established and headquartered in Tashkent, where US built a K-2 Karshi-Khanabad airbase after September 11 terrorist attacks but withdrew after 2004 Velvet Revolution in Georgia. Russian leaders have not hidden their desire to drive the United States out of Central Asia. Moscow, for instance, was instrumental in getting the Shanghai Cooperation Organization to adopt an early July resolution that called on the United States to set a deadline for withdrawal from air bases in both Uzbekistan and Kyrgyzstan. In making the call, Russian officials contended that Afghanistan is stabilizing, thus eliminating the strategic rationale for the continuing presence of American forces in Central Asia.[6]

---

[6] Uzbekistan Serves United States with Air Base Eviction Notice. July 31, 2005. http://www.eurasianet.org/departments/insight/articles/eav080105.shtml

Table 2: Annual Summit of SCO

SCO Documents[7] of Annual Meetings of States Members and Heads of Governments	
Annual Summit	Important Documents and Action Agendas
2001 Shanghai, China	1. Statement of the Heads of Governments of the Member States of Shanghai Cooperation Organization 2. Declaration of the Creation of the Shanghai Cooperation Organization 3. Shanghai Convention 4. Joint Statement of Heads of State of the Republic of Kazakhstan, China, Kyrgyzskoy Republic, the Russian Federation, Tajikistan, Uzbekistan
2002 St.Petersburg, Russia	1. Joint Communiqué of the meeting of the Council of Ministers of Foreign Affairs of the SCO Member States 2. TIME CHART relationship Shanghai Cooperation Organization with other international organizations and states 3. Statement of Ministers of Foreign Affairs of the member States of the Shanghai Cooperation Organization 4. Declaration of Heads of States of the Shanghai Cooperation Organization 5. Charter of the Shanghai Cooperation Organization 6. Joint Statements of the Foreign Ministers of States Parties to the Shanghai Cooperation Organization

---

[7] http://www.sectsco.org/RU/index.asp
http://www.sectsco.org/EN/

2003 Moscow, Russia	1. Joint Communiqué of the meeting of the Council of Heads of Government (Prime Ministers) of Shanghai Cooperation Organization 2. Joint Communiqué of the extraordinary meeting of the Council of Ministers of Foreign Affairs of the SCO Member States 3. Declaration of Heads of States of the Shanghai Cooperation Organization
2004 Tashkent, Uzbekistan	1. Joint Communiqué of the Council of Heads of Government (Prime Ministers) of Shanghai Cooperation Organization 2. Tashkent Declaration of Heads of State of the Shanghai Cooperation Organization 3. The Regulations on Observer Status at the Shanghai Cooperation Organization
	Cooperation Organization
2005 Astana, Kazakhstan	1. Protocol on Establishment of the SCO-Afghanistan Contact Group betweeen the Shanghai Cooperation Organisation and the Islamic Republic of Afghanistan 2. Joint Communiqué of the meeting of the Council of Heads of Government / Prime Ministers / SCO 3. Declaration of the Heads of State of the Shanghai cooperation Organization 4. Joint Communiqué meeting of the Council of Foreign Ministers - the Shanghai cooperation Organization
2006 Shanghai, China	1. Joint Communiqué of Meeting of the Council of the Heads of the Member States of the Shanghai Cooperation Organisation 2. Declaration on the Fifth Anniversary of the Shanghai Cooperation Organization

	Cooperation Organization
2007 Bishkek, Kyrgyztan	1. Chronicle of main events at SCO in 2007 2. Joint Communiqué of Meeting of the Council of Heads of Member States of the Shanghai Cooperation Organisation 3. Bishkek Declaration of the Heads of the Member States of the Shanghai Cooperation Organisation 4. Treaty on Long-Term Good-Neighborliness, Friendship and Cooperation Between the Member States of the Shanghai Cooperation Organization 5. Memorandum of Understanding between the Secretariat of the SCO and the CSTO 6. Informational Announcement for the meeting of the Council of foreign Ministers of SCO Member States
2008 Dushanbe, Tajikistan	1. Chronicle of main events at SCO in 2008 2. Joint Communiqué of Meeting of the Council of the Heads of the Member States of the Shanghai Cooperation Organisation 3. Dushanbe Declaration of the Heads of the Member States of the Shanghai Cooperation Organisation 4. Regulations on the Status of Dialogue Partner of the Shanghai Cooperation Organisation
2009 Yekaterinburg, Russia	1. Chronicle of main events at SCO in 2009 2. Joint Statement on fighting against infectious diseases in the region of the Shanghai Cooperation Organisation 3. SCO Joint Initiative on increasing multilateral economic cooperation in the field of tackling the consequences of the global financial economic crisis

俄羅斯再次崛起？──雙頭鷹的亞太政策與戰略思想

	4. Joint Communique of Meeting of the Council of the Heads of Government (Prime Ministers) of the SCO Member States 5. Joint Communiqué of Meeting of the Council of the Heads of the Member States of the Shanghai Cooperation Organisation 6. Yekaterinburg Declaration of the Heads of the Member States of the Shanghai Cooperation Organisation 7. Statement by the Shanghai Cooperation Organization Member States and the Islamic Republic of Afghanistan on combating terrorism, illicit drug trafficking and organized crime 8. Plan of Action of the Shanghai Cooperation Organization Member States and the Islamic Republic of Afghanistan on combating terrorism, illicit drug trafficking and organized crime 9. Declaration of the special Conference on Afghanistan convened under the auspices of the Shanghai Cooperation Organization
2010 Tashkent, Uzbekistan	1. Chronicle of main events at SCO in 2010 2. Cooperation between the United Nations and the Shanghai Cooperation Organization 3. Declaration of the Tenth Meeting of the Council of the Heads of the Member States of the Shanghai Cooperation Organisation 4. Joint Communiqué of the Tenth Meeting of the Council of the Heads of the Member States of the Shanghai Cooperation Organisation 5. Joint Communique of Meeting of the Council of the Ministers of Foreign Affairs of the SCO Member States 6. Joint Declaration on SCO/UN Secretariat Cooperation

2011 Astana, Kazakhstan	1. Astana Declaration of the 10th Anniversary of the Shanghai Cooperation Organisation 2. Joint Communiqué of meeting of the Council of the Heads of the Member States of the Shanghai Cooperation Organisation commemorating the 10th anniversary of the SCO
2012 Beijing, China	1. The Declaration of Heads of SCO Member States on the construction of the region of lasting peace and common prosperity 2. The Resolution on the Strategic Plan of the SCO development for the medium term 3. The resolution of the Statutes of the political and diplomatic measures and mechanisms to respond to the SCO situation that endangers peace, security and stability in the region 4. The resolution of the Program of cooperation in combating terrorism, separatism and extremism for 2013-2015 years 5. The resolution on the report of the SCO Secretary General on the activities of the SCO in the past year 6. The resolution on the report of the Board of the Regional Antiterrorist Structure (RATS) activity in 2011 7. The resolution on granting observer status to Afghanistan in the organization 8. The resolution to grant Turkey the status of dialogue partner 9. The resolution of the SCO Secretary General and Director of the resolution of the Executive Committee of the RATS SCO

Soon after the terrorist attacks on the United States on September 11, 2001, all the Central Asian "front-line" states offered over-flight and other support for coalition anti-terrorism operations in Afghanistan. Kyrgyzstan, Tajikistan, and Uzbekistan hosted coalition troops and provided access to airbases. In 2003, Kazakhstan and Uzbekistan also endorsed coalition military action in Iraq. About two dozen Kazakhstani troops served in Iraq until late 2008. Uzbekistan rescinded U.S. basing rights in 2005 after the United States criticized the reported killing of civilians in the town of Andijon. In early 2009, Kyrgyzstan ordered a U.S. base in that country to close, allegedly because of Russian inducements and U.S. reluctance to meet Kyrgyz requests for greatly increased lease payments. An agreement on continued U.S. use of the Manas Transit Center was reached in June 2009. In recent years, most of the regional states also participate in the Northern Distribution Network for the transport of U.S. and NATO supplies into and out of Afghanistan. [8] (Jim Nichol, 2012)

SCO: Russia's Eurasian Geopolitics and Energy Security Strategy

Geopolitics is in. From Beijing to Delhi, Berlin and Paris, geopolitics is now widely used by statesmen, political analysts, and scholars alike. The precise meaning of geopolitics can vary greatly. Analysts and journalist are prone to use the term as simply a synonym for power politics. But for most, geopolitics implies a geographical imperative that in some way conditions patterns of national politics and

---

[8] (Jim Nichol, 2012) Central Asia: Regional Developments and Implications for U.S. Interests, Congressional Research Service, 7-5700, www.crs.gov, RL33458.

international relations. It suggests at a minimum that the geography of states-size, location, topography, natural conditions, resource endowment, and so on-is critical in determining both their historical evolution and their prospects for future development. In the past, scholars of geopolitics expressed this imperative as simple axioms that were supposed to determine the fates of great states over the long run. Today's geopoliticians are more inclined to be careful, expressing the geographical imperative as multivariate and probabilistic (and therefore less easily falsifiable) propositions. Still, at its root, geopolitics posits that location matters, and matters decisively in the long run.[9] (William C. Wohlforth , 2006)

Russia's multipolar policy consumed a great deal of the foreign ministry's and the president's energy, most notably during Putin's first year in office. The rhetoric surrounding it was loud and consistent. And the policy of wooing other continental great powers like China, India, France, and Germany was supplemented by a far more controversial strategy of courting regional U.S. adversaries like Iran and Iraq. While the overall policy could be explained partly by reference to a number of potential near-term benefits-a diplomatic bargaining ploy, a popular move with domestic constituencies, a result of incoherent policymaking institutions, an effort driven by commercial interest and the defense-industrial complex-it was consistent enough to suggest a mild version of the geopolitical heartland logic at work. That is, the policy reflected a belief that Russia could serve as a key broker in fashioning policy

---

[9] Wolfgang Danspeckgruber (2006) Perspectives on the Russian State in Transition, Princeton University. (William C. Wohlforth (2006) "HEARTLAND DREAMS:Russian Geopolitics and Foreign Policy":265-267.)

coalitions, not power-aggregating alliances, among major Eurasian states in opposition to the United States. Although this strategy was a shadow of the strong geopolitical language used to describe it, its outlines did correspond to the geopolitical premises that inform so much recent Russian thinking.[10] (William C. Wohlforth, 2006)

Russia has always had an ambiguous relationship with Asia. By reason of its eastward expansion from the 16th century onwards, it incorporated a third of the Asian landmass into what was by culture and history a European country. In both the imperial and communist eras the predominant Russian perceptions of Asia remained rooted in European culture, including the officially sanctioned ideologies of the time. The imperialism of the 19th century and the Marxism-Leninism of the 20th were both derived from Russia's involvement in the European state and class system.[11]

However, consciousness of Russia's singular position between Europe and Asia, and the implications of this for its social development and external orientation, has also been a constant element in Russian political culture. There was an inherent element of geographic, as well as cultural, distinctiveness within the Slavophile movement of the 19th century, though this did not imply any preference for Asiatic culture

---

[10] Wolfgang Danspeckgruber (2006) Perspectives on the Russian State in Transition, Princeton University. (William C. Wohlforth (2006) HEARTLAND DREAMS: Russian Geopolitics and Foreign Policy:277.)

[11] For interpretations of Russian perspectives on Asia in the imperial and communiste rassee N.V. Riasanovsky, 'Asia through Russian Eyes', in Wayne Vucinich(ed), Russiaand Asia(Stanford, CA, Hoover Institution Press, 1972); John J. Stephan, 'Asia in the Soviet Conception', in Donald S. Zagoria(ed), Soviet Policy in East Asia (London, Yale University Press, 1982); Mark Mancall, Russia and China: Their Diplomatic Relations to 1728 (London, 1971).

over European culture. The primary reasons for the strengthening of the geopolitical character of the Eurasian concept from the beginning of the 20th century were the changes in the international order, including, in East Asia, the decline of Russia's long-term partner, China, and the rise of Japan. Russian expansion eastward had been driven by the traditional aims of imperialism-economic gain and territorial security-in which it had been markedly successful throughout most of the 18th and 19th centuries. With the demise of the Qing and the defeat by Japan, however, the prospect that the East might pose a threat to Russia, as it had in the pre-modern era, arose once more. The degree to which geopolitical concerns did shape Soviet foreign policy and 979 DAVID KERR military doctrine during the Cold War only became open for discussion in the last years of the Soviet Union.[12] (David Kerr, 1995)

Central Asia is one of the world's most energy-rich regions. According to a 2008 BP energy survey, the five nations bordering the Caspian Sea-Azerbaijan, Iran, Kazakhstan, Turkmenistan, and Russia--plus Uzbekistan hold roughly 21.4 percent of the world's proven oil reserves and 45 percent of the world's proven natural gas reserves. In recent years, SCO member states have sought greater energy cooperation. At a 2007 summit, former Russian president and current Prime Minister Vladimir Putin called for an "energy dialogue, integration of our national energy concepts, and the creation of an energy club" (Eurasianet). During that meeting, member states agreed to establish a "unified energy market" for oil and gas exports, while also promoting regional development through preferential energy agreements. Some

---

[12] David Kerr (1995) The New Eurasianism: The Rise of Geopolitics in Russia's Foreign Policy, Europe-Asia Studies, Vol. 47, No. 6: 978-980

experts are concerned that a potential SCO gas cartel would pose a significant threat, especially if Iran attained full membership. "It would essentially be an OPEC with bombs," David Wall, a regional expert at the University of Cambridge's East Asia Institute, told the *Washington Times* in 2006.[13] (Andrew Scheineson, 2009)

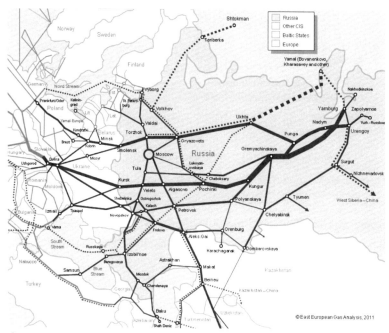

◆Figure 1: Russia's Natural Gas Pipelines

http://www.eegas.com/fsu.htm

---

[13]Andrew Scheineson (2009) The Shanghai Cooperation Organization」. The Council on Foreign Relations (CFR) http://www.cfr.org/international-peace-and-security/shanghai-cooperation-organization/p10883

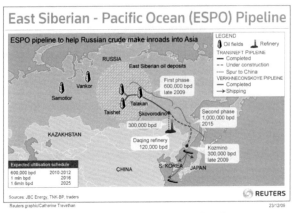

◆Figure 2: Eastern Siberian-Pacific Ocean Pipeline

Over the last several years, the view has grown that the power to ensure access to international energy resources has shifted away from energy consumers to energy producers. The growth of China and India as large consumers of energy, coupled with an inability to develop reliable and affordable alternatives to oil and natural gas, has led to this development. In December 2005-January 2006, when Russia dramatically raised the price of natural gas that it was supplying to Ukraine, many saw an effort to squeeze Ukraine politically and economically to secure Kiev within Russia's orbit. Moscow's effort also underscored the shift towards the ability of energy producers to exert pressure on countries dependent upon them for supplies.[14] (Bernard Gelb, Jim Nichol, and Steven Woehrel, 2006)

---

[14]Bernard Gelb, Jim Nichol and Steven Woehrel (2006). Russia's Cutoff of Natural Gas to Ukraine: Context and Implications, CRS Report RS22378:1-6.

俄羅斯再次崛起？──雙頭鷹的亞太政策與戰略思想

The United States and its European allies have begun to discuss the appropriate institutions and policies for ensuring energy security. The Bush Administration introduced a discussion of energy security at NATO in February 2006, with the support of key allies such as Britain and Germany. At the same time, EU governments view energy security in a broad manner, and most believe that political and economic measures are the first steps to ensure access to energy resources. Most EU members are also members of NATO, and energy security may emerge as an issue handled in a complementary manner by the two organizations.[15] (Paul Gallis2006)

"Energy diplomacy" has experienced a vivid renaissance during the last decade. It is particularly the newest consumers that tend to resort to bilateral deals and diplomacy when it comes to securing supply. Yet, while strengthening planning security on produced and contracted volumes, this risk hedging arrangement obviously comes with a cost: it levers out the price mechanism. This has an important consequence as the price mechanism plays no role in valuing "energy security." In theory, some consumers may highly value supply security and are willing to spend money now, thus improving their future security situation. Others may put more value on present consumption and regard potential future supply disruptions as a risk they are willing to accept and for whose mitigation they are not willing to pay. Yet, to the extent the individual "valuation" of energy security is concerned, the price-peg in prevalent gas market arrangements renders price signals meaningless. In fact, it prevents differing preferences from being catered.

---

[15] Paul Gallis (2006). "NATO and Energy Security", CRS Report RS22409:1-6.

No European consumer can effectively account for his individual degree of risk aversion and pay less or more for energy security in gas supplies.[16] (Andreas Goldthau, 2012)

Russia, one of the world's two energy superpowers, is rich in natural energy resources. It has the largest known natural gas reserves of any state on earth, along with the second largest coal reserves, and the eighth largest oil reserves. Russia is the world's fourth largest electricity producer after the USA, China, and Japan. Russia exports 70% of oil produced, about 7 million of 10.12 million barrels (1,609,000 m^3) a day (2010), the largest net oil export of any country, as well as a major supply to the European Union. The entire Middle East, in comparison, exports 20 million barrels (3,200,000 m^3) daily.[17] The Energy policy of Russia is contained in an Energy Strategy document, which sets out policy for the period up to 2020. In 2000 the Russian government approved the main provisions of the Russian energy strategy to 2020, and in 2003 the new Russian energy strategy was confirmed by the government. The Energy Strategy document outlines several main priorities: an increase in energy efficiency, reducing impact on the environment, sustainable development, energy development and technological development, as well as improved effectiveness and competitiveness.

The first oil pipeline linking the world's biggest oil producer, Russia, and the world's biggest consumer of energy, China, has begun operating in 2010. The pipeline, running between Siberia and the northeastern Chinese city of Daqing, will allow a rapid increase in oil exports between

[16] Andreas Goldthau (2012)." A Public Policy Perspective on Global Energy Security", International Studies Perspectives (2012) 13, 65–84.
[17] http://www.thomaswhite.com/explore-the-world/russia. aspx#recent

the two countries. Russian oil has been transported to China by rail. Concentrated in western Siberia, Russia's network of pipelines for oil exports has so far run towards Europe. Russia is expected to export 15m tonnes of oil through the new pipeline each year during the next two decades-about 300,000 barrels a day. The project cost $25bn (£16bn) and was partly financed by Chinese loans. Russia overtook Saudi Arabia as the world's largest oil producer in 2009. China surpassed the US as the world's largest consumer of energy last year. A second stage of construction on the pipeline is due to be finished by 2014. It will then span a distance of about 4,700 kms.[18]

Russia regards the energy as the strategic recourse but not merely the commercial goods. The state-run energy company Gazprom plays the role of bargaining. The oil pipeline from Angarsk to Daqing was proposed to establish in 2003, but with the fighting for pipelines between Japan and China, the starting point was turned to be Taishet. It seems that Russia could wait for the beneficial proposal with patience. China's part of the oil pipeline was financed by the Chinese government herself and the loan will be used for the future payment. However, Russia's opinions shows that the public is not satisfied with the low prices and China's public opinions show that Russia delayed the construction timing and later raising the oil prices that has damaged the mutual trust between these two countries' friendship. So for energy security, China also hopes to diversify the oil supply sources. China's role in SCO is embarrassed because China relies on Russia's and CIS members' energy and under the framework of SCO China could only invest huge capital

---

[18] Russia-China oil pipeline opens, 2 January 2011, BBC News Asia-pacific.
http://www.bbc.co.uk/news/world-asia-pacific-12103865

to improve the stability of the energy supply sources. China now is seriously thinking about her energy policy or she will face the crisis of future economic transformation.

US Factors' Influence on SCO

2012 Beijing the 12th Anniversary SCO Summit has its significance because time by time SCO has become the influential regional organization. Both China and Russia doesn't want to be the enemies of USA but hope to balance their power after the global financial crisis. Russian analysis stressed the refusal of Iranian's membership application show the SCO's unwillingness to be seen as an anti-Western organization, since the US authority considers Iran's nuclear weapons' plan has endangered the security of the United States and has put the sanctions on Iran into work. China attempts to vast its economic influence in Central region and insists on the principles of territorial dignity and anti-terrorism and separatism as whole of the principles when facing the border disputes and regional separatism. China has been poor and weak for a long time and prefers to be the economic power to increase China's image and the national self-confidence of the Chinese people in the world.

Russia cares about the stable regime and the drugs and terrorism which have endangered the national security and damaged the prestige of the regime in Russia. Putin came back as the security saver but didn't imitate the Western democratic paradigm. Putin has paid more attention to broadening his diplomatic influence on the international intervention as part of his global strategy for pursuing the super power status again. Russia has expressed her opposition toward the unilateral resolution by the United States but is not able to confront them by herself. Russia shows her traditional independent diplomacy to maintain her national interests and it's very important to know that the Russian political thoughts and ideology of anti-imperialism remain functioning from the past. Russia's diplomacy is preventive than aggressive but using the confrontation as the negotiation approaches and bargaining chips. Russia believes that the independent diplomacy will enhance her global governance, brings benefits to her domestic economic interests and meet the psychological feelings of national security and national dignity as a whole.

The author assumes that Russia will strengthen her economic interests with China and India, and in this situation, Russia may not hope that China has military conflicts with the Asian countries. The SCO will not be the backup force for China, but Russia will express the opposite attitude toward China's military actions in Asian-Pacific region. Therefore, SCO might play the role of economic and strategic cooperation function but not the military alliance, because Russia needs to open the Asian energy market. Military confrontations in Asian-pacific region and establishing military alliance anti NATO doesn't cope with Russia's global governance and economic interests to broaden energy market if the United States lunch out economic sanctions and geopolitical containment. So producing the real Cold War confrontation is not beneficial for Russia's domestic development in the whole situation.

China is facing the challenges in the whole aspects. Now China is the second biggest economy but the per capita income is still in the low standard of the developing countries, because bureaucracy and corruption is eroding the society. In order to support the high GDP and industry, China needs the stable energy supplies from SCO members to reduce the risk of relying on the Iranian oil which are under the influence of USA's sanctions. China is afraid of US' economic sanctions and military intervention in the Asian-Pacific region. China also needs SCO consuming markets of the daily necessities. In this situation, Russia and China both has mutual economic interests, but China relies on Russia more than Russia relies on China, because after Russia becomes the 156th member of WTO, the diversified goods from the WTO members will reduce China's goods sold in Russia.

Therefore, China might follow Russia's international interventional actions and offend the United States' interests. This tendency of going closer to Russia will arouse the inner fight in the process of transformation of China's political regime. China's intelligentsia doesn't like this tendency but Chinese military will not be satisfied with the pro-US intelligentsia. The inner political fight in China will threaten the stability of new political regime. Now the Russia's independent foreign policy is very practical to help Putin's reforms but China's foreign policy has not formed because of the political fights. Therefore, SCO will not be developed into the military-aliened organization anti NATO but plays the role of negotiating the economic interests and confirming geopolitical strategy of security in Central Asia and in the Asian-Pacific region in the whole scale. We don't see that China could find the consensus in foreign policy but Russia is ready to enter Asia. If China and Russia could achieve the agreement for developing the energy markets, Russia' Asian-Pacific strategy will be successful. SCO could be very active actor in impacting the international system in the future years. The collective security and energy security strategy beyond the geopolitical conception for SCO will promote Russia to be the leader after the communism ideological camp collapsed and will also be effective actor in the post financial crisis era and Georgian war. So, will a new Cold War happen between Russia and the United States?

Will a New Cold War Happen?

Selbi Hanova assumes that the economic factor might plays the more important role in anti-western perception of SCO created for anti-enlargement of NATO. In fact, enhancement of the economic dimension of cooperation within the organization was frequently mentioned in many official documents of the organization, such as the 2002 SCO Charter and the Astana Declaration of 2005. However, closer examination of the comprehensive energy policies in the region might suggest that "multilateral agreement that integrates energy policy throughout the entire region is a difficult proposition, and that the agreements which have emerged are not products of the SCO, even if they are influenced by the SCO process." Rather, bilateral agreements between the member countries seem to be dominating, while the SCO serves as a context or framework for such agreements. For Russia it appears that EurAsEc (Eurasian Economic Community) and the CIS fulfill the role of concluding agreements.[19]

Obliviously, both China and Russia play the key roles in Central Asian region, which is transport hub between Asia and Europe. At the same time, SCO might play the multiple roles in energy supply, military defense and anti-terror criminal activities. The SCO has formed itself

---

[19] Selbi Hanova (2009) China and Eurasia Forum Quarterly, Volume 7, No. 3 (2009) : 63-81.

as a regional ally occupying the privilege in global governance and the ally will be usually connected and compared with the NATO. Under the pressure of NATO's expansion, SCO plays the role of mechanism of joint military exercises and recently the role of energy strategy which is rooted both in Central Asian region to meet Russia's Eurasian strategy and Asian-Pacific strategy after the 2008 global financial crisis.

We can see that Russia has launched his global political governance by establishing alliance such as SCO and BRICKS from its Asian-Pacific policy under Putin's new ruling regime in 2012. The establishment of Shanghai Cooperation Organization (SCO) is the result of that Russia and China hope to counterbalance the enhancing power of the United States in this region when the 911 terrorists attack accident occurred in 2001 and this event let the USA launch out the war into Afghanistan and Iraq. Russia and China felt the USA has intervened into the Central Asia and the Middle East. Therefore, these two countries were afraid of that the United States will take use of the anti-terrorist war to expand their military sphere for geopolitical containment. So Russia and China found the timing to establish the quasi-military cooperation organization to contend NATO's expansion in this region. To solve border deputes and oil price is also put into the agenda of SCO. So we can see that SCO is regarded as the mechanism to solve the problems of security which is related to the geopolitical competence, combating terrorism, defining border disputes and promoting energy supply.

The SCO reflects that both Russia and China feel isolated in regional integration and demands mutual trust in the future. Russia recognizes that she could not compete with China in economic area but Russia is able to be dominant by expanding membership to include Mongolia, India, Iran and Pakistan into SCO. In this situation, SCO will

俄羅斯再次崛起？──雙頭鷹的亞太政策與戰略思想

be the multilateral organization to contend the NATO in global political and military issues. In fact, China does not want to provoke USA to translate SCO as a real military organization but would like to enhance its economic and technological functions to maintain China's demands. Russia prefers SCO play more important role both in political but also in economic area for global governance. SCO plays more and more important role of geopolitical strategy in regional security and energy benefits. However, the controversial ideas between Russia and China remain strong.

The Perspective of SCO

Nicola P. Contessi thinks from the perspective of the organization's internal power relations, Russia appeared to have acquired a more prominent role, while China, the driving force behind the creation of the SCO, and its leading member in the years following its establishment appeared to have receded to a more discreet role. First, on the other hand, Russia has been boosting its profile in Central Asian security affairs throughout the year 2008-2009 even outside of the SCO. Second, reports suggest that as of 2006, China has allegedly shifted its interest to cooperation in the economic sphere. Moreover, China has traditionally been a cautious actor on the international scene, and the present international juncture may be suggesting the expediency of maintaining a low profile in the face of the financial crisis and security challenges on the home front. A further consideration may be that China is willing to appease Russia on the security front after refusing to endorse its August 2008 Georgian venture. The expansion of the SCO's areas of responsibility in recent years may have been dictated by this implicit deal. This could suggest that a more accurate reading of the current trend within the SCO may be of an emerging "division of labour" between the two powers in the context of a broader reframing of the organization's mandate and positioning.[20] (Contessi Nicola P., 2010)

Alyson J. K. Bailes and Pál Dunay think that established in 2001 with China, the Russian Federation, Kazakhstan, Kyrgyzstan, Tajikistan and Uzbekistan as members, the Shanghai Cooperation Organization (SCO) has remained one of the world's least-known and least-analyzed multilateral groups. It makes little effort itself for transparency and is only patchily institutionalized in any case. The SCO's founding documents already signaled the special interest of the member states in fighting what they defined as "terrorism, separatism and extremism." Security relevant areas are the most frequent subjects of working-level meetings, which now include experts on information security, secretaries of national security councils and heads of supreme courts.[21] (Alyson J. K. Bailes, Pál Dunay, Pan Guang and Mikhail Troitskiy, 2007)

Pan Guang who is the Director of the Shanghai Cooperation Organization Studies Center in Shanghai, the Shanghai Center for International Studies, and the Institute of European and Asian Studies at Shanghai Academy of Social Sciences think that the SCO provides a good framework for China to cooperate closely in combating terrorism, extremism, separatism and various other cross-border criminal forces. The primary target of the Chinese anti-terrorism campaign is the

---

[20] Contessi Nicola P. (2010) China and Eurasia Forum Quarterly, Volume 8, No. 4 (2010), pp. 101-123
[21] Alyson J. K. Bailes, Pál Dunay, Pan Guang and Mikhail Troitskiy(2007), The Shanghai Cooperation
Organization, SIPRI Policy Paper No.17, p1.

East Turkestan Islamic Movement (ETIM), which advocates the independence of Xinjiang and is said to be supported by Osama bin Laden. From the Chinese perspective, it is of particular importance that China has been able, in the SCO framework, to count on the support of the other nine member and observer states in its campaign against ETIM. Moreover, China has also been able to draw support from SCO partners in its efforts to frustrate other conventional or non-conventional security threats and to eliminate or ease the external factors of disruption to China's stability and development.[22]

Mikhail Troitskiy is an associate professor at Moscow State Institute of International Relations (MGIMO University) thinks, in the economic realm, Russia represents a moderating force vis-à-vis the ambitious Chinese free-trade agenda. Russia endorsed a framework agreement on enhanced economic cooperation among SCO member states in September 2003, and in September 2006 a Russian Foreign Ministry spokesman outlined an extensive list of joint economic projects that Russia would be interested in promoting through the SCO. These included expanding Eurasian telecommunications networks and a transport corridor to connect the Caspian Sea with China through Russia, Kazakhstan, Uzbekistan and Kyrgyzstan; developing agreements for exports of electrical power from states and regions with a surplus to interested SCO countries; and developing structures to coordinate trade in and transit of hydrocarbons among SCO member states, such as the SCO Energy Club that was proposed by Russian President Vladimir Putin at the Shanghai summit in June 2006. However, Russia's vision of the SCO's economic ambition falls short of creating the free-trade area

---

[22] Ibid, p. 46

that China called for at that summit. This controversy is discussed below in greater detail. The two countries have expanded bilateral trade and negotiated a number of deals in the energy field.[23]

Simbal Khan thinks that in March 2009, President Obama presented the draft of a new U.S. policy on Afghanistan and Pakistan, which aimed to address the security slide in Afghanistan with a spate of new strategies. One aspect of this new thinking was to address the increasing instability by addressing the regional dynamics and engaging the main regional actors. The SCO Special conference on Afghanistan was held in March 2009 in Moscow. The participation of Iran's Deputy Foreign Minister Mehdi Akhundzadeh along with the U.S. envoy at the conference was a testament to the fact that cooperation with the SCO offers the U.S. and NATO an acceptable format to bring Iran into the dialogue on Afghanistan. The SCO-Afghanistan Action Plan called for joint operations in combating terrorism, drug trafficking, organized crime, and for involving Afghanistan in a phased manner in SCO-wide collaboration in fighting terrorism in the region. The conference reiterated the SCO's known opposition to the expansion of U.S. military interests in Central Asia, but indicated its willingness to expand cooperation with the U.S. and NATO in Afghanistan albeit short of sending troops. Interestingly, President Obama announced a shift in U.S. policy emphasis on the same day as the SCO summit, promising greater consultation with Afghanistan's neighbors. Following this greater interaction, U.S./NATO have recently signed transit agreements with Russia and Central Asian states which allow for military and non-military supplies to transit their territories en route to Afghanistan.[24]

---

[23] Ibid, p. 32
[24] Khan Simbal(2009) China and Eurasia Forum Quarterly, Volume 7, No. 3: 11-15.

Deputy Secretary General of SCO Konarovskiy gave his remarks for the Third Ministerial Conference of the Paris Pact Partners held in Vienna on February 16, 2012. "Continuous armed conflict in Afghanistan caused a serious concern of the SCO member states. The region has not only become a major transit route but also turned into an expanding market for distribution and consumption of drugs of the Afghan origin. Drug trafficking, providing a significant financial support for the forces opposed to Kabul, can pose a serious threat to the stability and national security of the SCO nations. Countering drug trafficking from Afghanistan will remain the SCO's top priority in the short and medium term including the period after full withdrawal of foreign troops from that country. The Agreement on Cooperation in Combating Illicit Trafficking of Narcotic Drugs, Psychotropic Substances and Precursors of 17 June, 2004 laid legal foundations for joint actions by the SCO member states on combating drugs and drug-related crime in general."[25]

Alexander Lukin said In March 2009, a conference on Afghanistan was held in Moscow, in which the UN secretary-general and representatives of the Organization for Security and Cooperation in Europe took part. Now the SCO is playing an active role in solving the issue. He also said that the fight against drug trafficking is high on the SCO's agenda. Tajikistan had offered to create a center for fighting drug trafficking in a bid to prevent drugs from Afghanistan from being smuggled into other countries.[26]

---

[25] Remarks by M. Konarovskiy, Deputy Secretary General, Shanghai Cooperation Organization prepared for the Third Ministerial Conference of the Paris Pact Partners held in Vienna on February 16, 2012. http://www.sectsco.org/EN/show.asp?id=316
[26] Interest in working with SCO growing: expert. http://news.xinhuanet.com/english2010/indepth/2010-06/08/c_13338931_2.htm

Irina Kobrinskaya, an expert at the Russian Global Economy and International Affairs Institute, told Xinhua Agency on the eve of the 10th Anniversary SCO Tashkent summit that common interests inside the bloc include regional security, mainly in Afghanistan. On the one hand, people expect some really breathtaking prospective of the SCO as an economic alliance. On the other hand, the fact is that economic weights of SCO members are too different.[27]

Leonid Moiseev, the Russian President Dmitry Medvedev's special representative for SCO affairs, told Xinhua that When five years ago there was turbulence in Kyrgyzstan, the SCO helped to downgrade the level of adversity there. Now the situation in Kyrgyzstan is rather similar to that in 2005. The SCO plays its role again to decrease the tension on the borders, provide assistance to Kyrgyzstan. Another possible topic for the Tashkent summit would be the admission order for new members, the first time in the organization's history.[28]

According to the different viewpoints of experts and scholars, the perspectives of SCO might be concluded into several points:

1. The SCO area might be the huge labor supply and consuming market which will attract more foreign investment and infrastructure export into Eurasian and Asian-Pacific region, especially in Russia after the global financial crisis.

2. The strengthened SCO will help maintain the security for anti-terrorism. The western counties could breathe to recover their

---

[27] SCO Tashkent summit to focus on security, economic coordination. http://news.xinhuanet.com/english2010/world/2010-06/08/c_13339197_3.htm

[28] SCO Tashkent summit to focus on security, economic coordination. http://news.xinhuanet.com/english2010/world/2010-06/08/c_13339197_3.htm

economy. The collective security system of SCO will reduce the international criminals and the United States will focus on the economic transformation after the eight years invasion in Iraq and global financial crisis.

3. The SCO might be the cartel of energy. The stability in this region could provide the stable energy supplies. Nevertheless, Europe and China tries to diversify the energy sources and process the green energy strategy. The economic transformation will be the core elements of energy security.

The Problems of SCO

Some experts believe the strongest aspect of the SCO is that it is a convenient place for dialogue on security in Central Asia, including Afghan factors such as drug trafficking, terrorism, and organized crime. Currently, the SCO has been invited to every major international event related to Afghanistan.

Alexander Lukin, director for the Center for East Asia and SCO Studies at Moscow State University for International Relations, told Xinhua Agency that the SCO's development bank of foundation has still been on paper only. Now the member states consider creation of a special account for the multipartite projects. Until then, these projects will remain stranded. Interest in working with the SCO has been growing in the world, from the European Union to the United States. Lukin said that if the principles will be agreed, the issue of expansion could be mentioned. Iran and Pakistan, currently observers, applied to join, he said. "Besides, at the previous summit, new partners for dialogue had been introduced and given to Belarus and Sri Lanka. It shows the growing interest to the SCO in the world."[29]

Richard Weitz, a senior fellow and director of the Center for Political-Military Analysis at Hudson Institute. He is the author, among other works, of *Kazakhstan and the New International Politics of Eurasia*, thinks that the Shanghai Cooperation Organization (SCO) has yet to resolve the problem presented by Iran's efforts to become the institution's seventh full member. For the fourth consecutive year, existing SCO governments have declined to accept new full members or formal observers. Instead, the SCO has resorted to proliferating new categories of external association, producing a confusing hodgepodge of members, observers, "guests," and now "partners." Although SCO leaders say they are working on procedures to guide the organization's expansion, it seems that the SCO's major powers fail to agree on who should join and who should not.[30] Ruslan Y. Izimov who is Research Fellow of Department of Foreign Policy Studies, KISI under the President of the Republic of Kazakhstan, (Almaty, Kazakhstan), shares the same opinions about the range of expansion of SCO.[31]

Fazal UR-RAHMAN, Director of the Institute of China, Pakistan Strategical Research Center thinks that it is true that in every multilateral organization there are always one or two lead countries, which serve as the mainstay of that organization. In the case of SCO, China and Russia happened to be the core countries. It is also true that the success or

---

[29] SCO Tashkent summit to focus on security, economic coordination. http://news.xinhuanet.com/english2010/world/2010-06/08/c_13339197_3.htm

[30] Richard Weitz, 08/19/2009 issue of the CACI Analyst. http://www.cacianalyst.org/?q=node/5159

[31] http://www.siis.org.cn/Sh_Yj_Cms/Mgz/201202/2012711141511A3QW.DOC

failure of SCO would largely depend on the strategic cooperation or strategic competition between these two major players. It will not be out of place to suggest that SCO is a bipolar organization and would need a fine balance between the two key players to be effective and to achieve its objectives.[32]

Wu Fei, the researcher on international issues of Guangdong Provincial government and the associate professor of Guangzhou JiNan University thinks, if SCO turns to be an organization of energy, it will arouse the tension from USA and impact the uprising of China. China and India both get benefit in the trend of globalization, and China is promoting the political reform. Democracy and national interest will be the core of US foreign affairs. China using SCO as the approach of getting energy will affect US and NATO energy interest and anti-terrorism operation. China will pay more cost with the relations with the Unite Sates of America.[33]

Several problems of SCO for China will be discussed as following:

1. Military union: the Shanghai Cooperation Organization (SCO) units China, Russia and the Central Asian countries, every state member has its own national interests and attitudes toward the military cooperation. China remains to need Russia's military support both in

---

[32] Fazal UR-RAHMAN (2008)SCO: Problems of enhancing economic cooperation.
http://www.eurasiacritic.com/articles/sco-problems-enhancing-economic-cooperation
[33] Wu Fei (2006) · Should China use SCO for searching energy, Takungpao daily newspaper, HK · 2006/6/28.

strategic and technological aspect. China has the territorial disputes with its neighbors and facing the threat from Japan's militarism and Taiwan's independence. SCO is the framework to cooperate with Russia. At the same time with the threat of North Korea's nuclear weapons, Russia plays the key role in China's decisions.

2. National security: all the members are facing the same problems of terrorism and separatism. The security problem will have impact on the national stability and economic development in the west area of China. China regards the terrorism in central Asia as the main source of terrorism connected with the Turkestan Islamic Movement (ETIM) in Xinjiang. The anti-terrorism cooperation with the central Asian states should be strengthened. The situation in Afghanistan is cared after US' troops withdraw from Afghanistan.

3. Economic interests: China needs the energy import from Russia, Central Asia and Middle East countries. The building of oil pipelines will provide long-term and stable resources for China. The energy cartel in SCO will make the international oil market prices controlled and monopolized by SCO. Russia also plays the key role in energy sales.

4. Neighboring relations：The problem is that China views SCO as its energy and military provider and at the same time as the security umbrella for developing economy and balancing US-Japan union in the eastern Asian region. SCO will be regarded as the similar military union against NATO. It's intransparency will arose doubt from the west countries. China wants to highlight its international status especially in Asian-Pacific by replacing US after the 2008 global financial crisis. The tension between China and US will not benefit China.

5. Interests conflicts: For Russia, SCO should be the base of enlarging cooperation with the Asia-Pacific region . If China cannot enlarge

the free trade cooperation range for the SCO members and make the agreement for the oil prices, there will be neither prospect of SCO in economic prosperity nor military trust between Russia and China. If the direction and function cannot be confirmed, the function of SCO must be weakened.

6. Direction of SCO: Iran's nuclear program has aroused US' sanctions. The relationship with Iran is very sensitive. The Shanghai Cooperation Organization (SCO) has yet to resolve the problem presented by Iran's efforts to become the institution's seventh full member. For the fourth consecutive year, existing SCO governments have declined to accept new full members or formal observers. Instead, the SCO has resorted to proliferating new categories of external association, producing a confusing hodgepodge of members, observers, "guests," and now "partners. " Although SCO leaders say they are working on procedures to guide the organization's expansion, it seems that the SCO's major powers fail to agree on who should join and who should not.

Conclusion

Nevertheless, SCO has become a quasi-military alliance for collective security and energy cartel monopoly with combining Russia, China and Central Asian countries. So Russia is forming her led-groups by the energy and high-tech weapons market to broaden her trade market. The collective organizations such as CIS, CIS CSTO, EAEC or EurAsEC, SCO and BRICS are forming time by time after the collapse of USSR, Russia's foreign policy and global strategy has changed from unifying the former USSR States under the loose framework of CIS to a global alliance such as SCO and BRICS by establishing the collective security mechanism and Eurasian economic community with the Central Asian countries to consolidate the CIS alliance, organizing SCO to strengthen the regional collective security into Asian-Pacific and Middle East, and developing BRICS to participate in the global governance and international intervention. SCO has more the strategic function than the military value. Russia will take use of negotiating and cooperating approach to recover her international status instead of military and ideological confrontations which were formed in the Cold War period. However, the influence of SCO on international security issues is going up and Russia attempts to process negotiations with the western countries under the framework UN Security Council and this will enhance Russia' international status and power. So Russia must oppose the unipolarity of the United States and advocate for going back to the UN institute. This bipolarity between Russia and the United States under the UN Security Council is forming and China often plays the key role in this triangle relations.

References

1. Ajami, F. (1993) The Summoning, Foreign Affairs 72(4):2–9.

2. Alhajji, A.F. (2007) What Is Energy Security? Definitions And Concepts. Middle East Economic Survey:39-45.

3. Alyson J. K. Bailes, Pál Dunay, Pan Guang and Mikhail Troitskiy (2007), The Shanghai Cooperation Organization, SIPRI Policy Paper No. 17.

4. Askar Akaev(2004), Relations with Russia Are a Priority, International Affairs 6 : 88-94.

5. Bernard Gelb, Jim Nichol, and Steven Woehrel (2006). Russia's Cutoff of Natural Gas to Ukraine: Context and Implications, CRS Report RS22378:1-6.

6 Bogaturove A. (1992), Vneshnyayap olitikaR ossii, SShA, 10: 27.

7. Bogaturov A. (1993) The Eurasian Support of World Stability, I nternational Affairs (Moscow), February: 41.

8. Chen Ou (2011), Russian Political Challenges on China's Security during Hu Jintao's Age, Asian Social Science 7: 79-85.

9. Cohen Saul B. (1963) Geography and Politics in a World Divided, New York: Random House, See especially, Dugin, Osnovy geopolitki :Fundamentals of geopolitics.

10. Contessi Nicola P. (2010) China and Eurasia Forum Quarterly, Volume 8, No. 4 (2010), pp. 101-123

11. David Kerr (1995) The New Eurasianism: The Rise of Geopolitics in Russia's Foreign Policy, Europe-Asia Studies, Vol. 47, No. 6:977-988.

12. Emad El-Din Aysha(2003) Samuel Huntington and the Geopolitics of American Identity: The Function of Foreign Policy in America's

Domestic Clash of Civilizations, International Studies Perspectives 4:113-132.

13. Fazal UR-RAHMAN (2008) SCO: Problems of enhancing economic cooperation.

14. Gallis Paul (2006). NATO and Energy Security, CRS Report RS22409:1-6.

15. Goldthau, A. (2010) Energy Diplomacy in Trade and Investment of Oil and Gas. In Global Energy Governance. The New Rules of the Game, edited by A. Goldthau and J.M. Witte. Washington, DC:Brookings Press.

16. Goldthau A. (2012) A Public Policy Perspective on Global Energy Security, International Studies Perspectives (2012) 13: 65–84.

17. Gregory Gleason & Marat E. Shaihutdino(2005) Collective Security and Non-State Actors in Eurasia, International Studies Perspectives (2005) 6: 274-284.

18. Jim Nichol (2012) Central Asia: Regional Developments and Implications for U.S. Interests, Congressional Research Service, 7-5700, www.crs.gov, RL33458.

19. Johnson, R. H. (1997) Impossible Dangers: U.S. Concepts of Threat in the Cold War and After, New York: St.Martin's Press.

20. Jonathan Sullivan & Bettina Renz, 'Chinese migration: still the major focus of Russian Far East/Chinese North East relations?' (2010), Pacific Review 23: 261-85.

21. Khan Simbal(2009) China and Eurasia Forum Quarterly, Volume 7, No. 3: 11-15.

22. Kissinger, H. A. (1994) Diplomacy. London: Simon and Schuster.

23. Likhachev V.L. (2010) The Shanghai Cooperation Organization and energy cooperation: current status and development prospects. sei.irk.ru›symp2010/en/papers/ENG/P1-07e.pdf

24. Macnamara, J. (2005). Media content analysis: Its uses, benefits and Best Practice
    Methodology. Asia Pacific Public Relations Journal, 6(1): 1-34.

25. Neuendorf, K. (2002) The Content Analysis Guidebook, Thousand Oaks, CA: Sage Publications.

26. Huntington, S.P. (1998) the Clash of Civilizations and the Remaking of World Order. London: Touchstone Books.

27. Hung Nguyen (1993) Russia and China: Genesis of an Eastern Rapallo, Asian Survey, Vol. 33, No. 3, March 1993, p. 286.

28. Richard Weitz, 08/19/2009 issue of the CACI Analyst.
    http://www.cacianalyst.org/?q=node/5159

29. Russia Beyond the Headlines.
    http://rbth.ru/articles/2009/01/21/210109_sco.html

30. Selbi Hanova (2009) China and Eurasia Forum Quarterly, Volume 7, No. 3: 63-81.

31. Sonali Huria (2009) The Shanghai Cooperation Organization January 21, 2009,

32. Stern, J. (2007) Gas-OPEC: A Distraction from Important Issues of Russian Gas Supply to Europe.Oxford Energy Comment 2.

33. Thoraas Rawski (2012) Japan's Economic Relations with China, Russia, and India: An Introductio', Eurasian Geography & Economics 53: 419-21.

34. Richard Weitz, 'Superpower Symbiosis:The Russia-China Axis' , World Affairs 175 (2012), 71-8.

35. Vladimir Portyakov (2006) Russia and Beyond. Russia, China and India in the World Economy, Russia in Global affairs 2: 124-30.

36. Vlahos, M. (1991) Culture and Foreign Policy, Foreign Policy 82(Spring):59-78.

37. Wolfgang Danspeckgruber (2006) Perspectives on the Russian State in Transition, Princeton University . (William C. Wohlforth (2006) "HEARTLAND DREAMS:Russian Geopolitics and Foreign Policy": 265-281.)

38. Wu Fei (2006) Should China use SCO for searching energy, Takungpao daily newspaper, HK, 2006/6/28.

39. Yergin, D. (2006) Ensuring Energy Security. Foreign Affairs 85 (2): 69-82.

40. Zagorsky A.(1994) Russia, the CIS and the West', International Affairs (Moscow), December : 65.

41. The official website of Shanghai Cooperation Organization (SCO)

42. http://www.globalsecurity.org/military/world/int/sco.htm

43. http://www.sco-ec.gov.cn/crweb/scor/info/Article.jsp?col_no=321&a_no=56546

44. http://www.sco-ec.gov.cn/crweb/scor/info/Article.jsp?col_no=321&a_no=56545

45. http://en.wikipedia.org/wiki/Shanghai_Cooperation_Organisation

46. http://www.siis.org.cn/Sh_Yj_Cms/Mgz/201202/2012711141511A3QW.DOC

North Korea's Crisis:

How Does Russia Look

at the Kim Jong-Un's Regime?[*]

Just at 4 o'clock on March 29 in Pyongyang, Kim Jong-Un signed an order on the plan to strike the territory of the United States probably for responding to the ongoing and routine U.S.-ROK military exercises from March 1 to April 30. Concerning of the DPRK's military threats to the North-East Asia, Russia has her own consideration of national security and interests.

Russia's Position from Minister of Foreign Affairs

The Minster of the Foreign Affairs of the Russian Federation Sergey Lavrov said the concern of the reactions from the Security Council and the world community on this event is unipolar action which might escalate the military tension. We should not use this event as the excuse of any geopolitical missions or we would lose the control and slip into the spiral of vicious circle.[1]

Russian Foreign Minister Sergei Lavrov said North Korea's nuclear test deserves condemnation and a reaction from the UN Security Council. He also said the six-party talks on the nuclear problem of the Korean peninsula must be restarted soon. "This [nuclear test] must be condemned. It demonstrates that the North Korean leadership has again

---

[*] The Author expresses the gratitude to Prof. Toloraya (Vice President of "Unity for Russia" Foundation), Prof. Victor Cha (Director of Asian Program at Georgetown University and Chair of Korea in the think tank of CSIS) and Prof. Wu Fei (Director of International Journalism and Communication of JiNan University) for their opinions in author's meeting with them. The paper only reflects the author's own opinion and doesn't reflect their attitude toward the issue.

[1] See "Putin and Kim Jong-un Scared Half of the World." (Владимир Путин и Ким Чен Ын напугали полмира) http://tvrain.ru/articles/vladimir_putin_i_kim_chen_yn_napugali_polmira-339912/

◆(Minister of Foreign Affairs of the Russian Federation – Sergei Lavrov. Photo source: EPA, the Voice of Russia)

◆(Kim Jong-Un signed an order putting rockets on stand-by after meeting generals.)

ignored international law and disregarded the UN Security Council's resolutions, all of which deserves condemnation and an adequate reaction. The UN Security Council will convene within hours to discuss this problem, I understand," Lavrov said at a press conference in Pretoria.[2]

Russian Foreign Minister Sergei Lavrov warned of a "vicious circle" and told all sides to avoid unilateral action. On Thursday, the North threatened to "settle accounts" and said it had put missiles on stand-by to hit the US. The US, which flew stealth bombers over South Korea this month, condemned the North's "bellicose rhetoric". White House spokesman Josh Earnest said the rhetoric only deepened North Korea's isolation. North Korean state media reported leader Kim Jong-Un "judged the time has come to settle accounts with the US imperialists".[3]

---

[2] See the news: "Russia to insist on soonest resumption of six-nation talks on North Korea –Lavrov." , February 12, 2013.
http://english.ruvr.ru/2013_02_12/Russia-to-insist-on-soonest-resumption-of-six-nation-talks-on-North-Korea-Lavrov/
[3] See the BBC news: "North Korea tensions: Russia's Lavrov fears 'spiral'", March 29, 2013.

"It was important for me to find out what the Americans thought about North Korea, and so when my counterpart was about to say goodbye after discussing the subject of Syria and raising no other subject, I said that it was also important to remain in contact on the problem, on the problem of the Korean Peninsula, in connection with the nuclear explosion that had been carried out by North Korea, and it was at my initiative that we discussed that issue," Lavrov said. He cited a Russian Foreign Ministry statement issued immediately after the test that condemned it as gross violation of a UN Security Council resolution, warned that there would be consequences for Pyongyang, but insisted on avoiding any military action in retaliation for the explosion. He reiterated that the purpose of the six-party talks is the denuclearization of the Korean Peninsula with security guarantees provided for all states in the region, including North Korea. "Russia and other negotiators stand ready to provide such guarantees, and we will be ready to work for their enshrinement in a decision by the UN Security Council," Lavrov said.[4]

Russia is Ready for the Multiple Talks

The director of Modern Korea Study Center of the Institute of World Economy and International Relations (IMEMO) George Toloraya believes that Kim Jong-Un hopes to begin negotiations with

---

http://www.bbc.co.uk/news/world-asia-21974381
[4] See the news "Lavrov, Kerry discussed North Korean nuclear test", February 18, 2013, *Interfax*.
http://rbth.ru/news/2013/02/18/lavrov_kerry_discussed_north_korean_nuclear_test_23012.html

Washington and Seoul. Toloraya served as the Economist-Representative in Pyongyang and Minister-Counselor in Seoul. He is also the Vice President of "Unity for Russia" Foundation (Russia ruling party think tank) and head of Regional Projects Department, Regional Director for Asia and Africa, "Russkiy Mir" Foundation.

In the interview *"Kim Jong-Un Dreams to Process Direct Negotiations with U.S.A"*[5], Toloraya answered the questions of radio *Voice of Russia* about the possible full-scale war in the Korean Peninsula. He said there might be war in accident but no one needs it at all. He described a young leader, who has not good skills to show the hopes to be treated well instead of being punished by isolations or sanctions, just like a dog being driven to the corner, it would bite. By his opinions, the aim of Kim's hysteria actions is to make the United States and South Korea compromise to start the talks. So, Toloraya thinks the most natural way to escape from the military conflict for peace is to begin the negotiations with North Korea and lure it from the unpredictable and hysteria situation.

According to his opinions, Moscow is worried about that some U.S. politicians and generals would take use of the North Korean threats to start a new allocation and build a missile defense shield, which is directed primarily against China and Russia. Concerning of the impact of possible war on Russian Far East, firstly it might be the nuclear power plants' reactor if the North Korea hit them in South Korea. What could

---

[5] See the interview by *the Voice of Russia*: "Kim Jong-Un Dreams to Process Direct Negotiations with U.S.A." (Георгий Толорая: "Ким Чен Ын мечтает провести прямые переговоры с США") http://rus.ruvr.ru/2013_03_29/Georgij-Toloraja-Kim-CHen-In-mechtaet-provesti-prjamie-peregovori-s-SSHA/

be the worst result? It might the biggest disaster in the 21st century.

Toloraya said it's hard to say how much influence that Russia might have on DPRK because this young leader studied in Switzerland and he might not be interested in Russian issues. His father Kim Jong Il was born in Russia and due to his warm feeling toward Russia, the Russian Center of Russkiy Mir Foundation was opened in Pyongyang. At 60% schools the Russian language are taught and it helped improve the relationships between Russia and North Korea. Toloraya said that it's hard to say how will be the relationship between these two counties under Kim Jong-Un's new regime. It will depend on the Russian diplomatic work.[6]

Toloraya said it not reality to ask for Kim to give up the nuclear and rocket programs totally but could give him opportunity to stop the uranium, plutonium and freeze the new construction of new reactors. He suggested that Obama administration is able to show the political willingness and financial aid for North Korea to establish this guarantee and conditions. This might give Kim Jong-Un to start the economic reforms to reduce the military conflicts and improve the security in this region. For Russia, it's important to ease the tension and promote the economy with North Korea.[7]

Why U.S. from the Bush administration to Obama administration is not hurry for talks?

---

[6] See the interview by the Russkiy Mir Foundation: "George Toloraya: In the Era of Kim Jong-un." (Георгий Толорая: В эпоху Ким Чен Ына). http://www.russkiymir.ru/russkiymir/ru/publications/interview/interview0226.html

[7] See the interview by the Russian newspaper *Russiskaya Gazeta* : "Russia Can Launch Satellites DPRK." (Россия может запускать спутники КНДР)
http://www.rg.ru/2012/12/16/zapusk-site.html

俄羅斯再次崛起？——雙頭鷹的亞太政策與戰略思想

Toloraya thought that the United States is playing the game of marginal war. He said: " At the same time initially North Koreans openly declared and called upon Russia and China to be witnesses -that they were prepared to make their nuclear program more transparent and even admit inspectors into the country, provided the U.S. give guarantees of inviolability (suggesting that in this case they will no longer need deterrence weapons). Washington, however, at this stage demonstrated no intentions to issue any guarantees; it declined to enter into negotiations with Pyongyang, despite pressure from Russia, China, and even Japan and South Korea. Paradoxically, as the crisis unraveled in the end of 2002- early 2003 US showed no marked signs of willingness to learn the truth about the North Korean nuclear program. Instead the US proposed bringing the discussion to the UN with an apparent hope to build a coalition against North Korea when the situation becomes more opportune. The North Koreans interpreted this as the U.S. playing a waiting game until the Iraqi campaign is over and took a new course- not only threatening with creation of nuclear weapons but making practical steps to produce it (it is important in this context that practical actions were taken by DPRK only after it declared walking out of NPT in January 2003)."[8]

Military Development is for Non-Military Goal?

The possible main concern is about Kim Jong-Un's consolidation of his power in DPRK. He might take use of the development of ballistic

---

[8] See the article of Toloraya: "Scenarios for North Korea."
http://world.lib.ru/k/kim_o_i/a971.shtml

missiles and anti-American actions to be the resolutions of the interior political fighting.

Russian Ambassador Gleb Ivashentsov thought that North Korea's action is understandable. The development of nuclear power and ballistic missiles is for the non-military goal. North Korean leader intends to implement independent national policy and obtain the financial aid for the reforms. The problem is not only the nuclear weapons but also their dissemination to other countries and organizations out of control. Russia tries to play the role of the bridge between ROK and DPRK for promoting the economic relationships with these two countries. Russia supports the style of six-talks to normalize the situation in Korean Peninsula.[9]

As Professor Victor Cha pointed out in his article "*Think Again: North Korea*" : Pyongyang conducted a third nuclear test in February, which appears to have been more successful than the previous two. Within President Barack Obama's second term in office, North Korea could well be the third nation (after Russia and China) to field a nuclear-tipped ballistic missile targeted at the United States. ...They need to read palace politics, reward friends and punish enemies, and manage competing interests that are vying for power... Signing a peace treaty in advance of denuclearization would recognize and legitimize Pyongyang's nuclear status, leaving it little incentive to shed those weapons. North Koreans have said to me that a peace treaty is just a piece of paper; why would they give up their cherished nuclear program for that?[10]

---

[9] See the interview by *The Epoch Times* : "Two wheels of a Cart or How to resolve the Korean Question." (Посол России Глеб Ивашенцов: Два колеса одной повозки, или как решать корейский вопрос)
http://www.epochtimes.ru/content/view/66927/54/

[10] See the article "Think Again; North Korea.", by David kang and Victor Cha. *Foreign Policy*, March 25, 2013.

俄羅斯再次崛起？──雙頭鷹的亞太政策與戰略思想

◆The critical importance of bilateral relations between China and Russia is evidently understood by both sides. Source: Konstantin Zavrazhin.

North Korea's Crisis Brings Russia and China Closer anti U.S.?

Chinese President Xi Jinping's first official visit to Moscow ended in over 30 economic agreements being signed, although the nature of the bilateral relationship is political, as well. China seeks a partner in the Asia-Pacific, where rhetoric on the "Chinese threat" is rising, and Russia wants political cooperation, which is lacking in its relations with the U.S. The critical importance of bilateral relations is evidently understood by both sides. Further proof is in the following passage from the joint statement issued after the talks on March 22-24 in Moscow: "Both countries will decisively support each other on issues relating to their core interests, including matters of sovereignty, territorial integrity, and security."[11]

---

http://www.foreignpolicy.com/articles/2013/03/25/think_again_north_korea
[11] See the article "China reaffirms strategic partnership in Russia." By Andrei Ilyashenko, special to *Russia Beyond the Headlines (RBTH)*,

China is North Korea's most important political and economic sponsor. However, its influence does not extend far enough to dissuade Pyongyang from conducting missile tests. However, for Beijing, this aborted exchange resulted in a loss of face. In response, China swiftly approved a set of UN sanctions against North Korea. The situation seems to be bringing Moscow and Beijing closer on the issue of countering U.S. missile defense. In May of last year, during the most recent summit of the Shanghai Cooperation Organization in Beijing, Russia and China, together with other members of the organization, condemned U.S. plans to deploy missile-defense shields in Europe and Asia. The Kremlin had already declared the missile shield in Europe to be a matter of national security. China, it seems, also harbors doubts that U.S. deployment of land and sea missile-defense components in Japan, Taiwan, South Korea, and the Philippines is related exclusively to North Korea's nuclear program.[12]

On March 7, the 15 members of United Nations Security Council unanimously passed a resolution 2094 on the DPRK recent move of the third nuclear test. North Korea on February 12 in this year processed the successful implementation of the third underground nuclear test. Prior to this, North Korea had conducted two nuclear tests in October 2006 and May 2009. The DPRK immediately said, will be a higher level of nuclear testing, for the protection of national autonomy to carry out

---

March 28, 2013.
http://rbth.ru/international/2013/03/28/china_reaffirms_strategic_partnership_in_russia_24385.html
[12] See the article "Tensions on the Korean peninsula bring Russia and China closer.", by Andrei Ilyashenko, special to *Russia Beyond the Headlines (RBTH)*, April 1, 2013.
http://rbth.ru/opinion/2013/04/01/moscow_and_beijing_need_to_flesh_out_security_concerns_24491.html

comprehensive decisive. [13]

Obviously, the sanctions would not make the regime give up his extreme approaches, and oppositely this would make the region more escalated and tensioned into the edge of war. Facing the isolation from the international community, Kim Jong-Un is playing the zero-sum games just like a crazy gambler. In this situation, the military confrontation and arms competition will be encouraged.

Russia and China supported the resolution was to show the world that they pursuit the goal of denuclearization of Korean Peninsula. For Russia, it's important to establish good relations both with ROK and DPRK for economic benefits and long-term strategic stability. For China, she doesn't want to take any responsibility for North Korea's confrontation with the United States. Both Russia and China needs to put the North Korea agenda into the UN system and this would strengthen their roles in participation in the future international affairs. However, neither Russia nor China really wants to take the sanctions seriously and implement the sanctions on North Korea, because they are worried about that this will push the Korean Peninsula into the edge of war out of their control.

As Sergei Lavrov assumed anyone who wants to use the event to achieve the geopolitical missions will escalate the military tensions, pushing the situation into the real war. This is very dangerous!

---

[13] See the article "The United Nations Security Council passed a sanctions resolution on North Korean nuclear test." http://ohsnapnews.com/the-united-nations-security-council-passed-a-sanctions-resolution-on-north-korean-nuclear-test/3783/

◆Drawing by Niyaz Karim.
http://nl.media.rbth.ru/web/en-rbth/files/china_russia_1536.jpg

後記

　　距離上次出書已經有兩年的時間了，再次感謝秀威出版社的支持，感謝他們對於俄羅斯這樣重要卻是銷路不廣的學術研究的鼓勵。

　　這段時間也產生了一些想法，這些想法與俄羅斯的政策變化和國家發展息息相關。撰寫的東西或許和從事的一些學術活動也密切關聯，包括了2011年到俄羅斯莫斯科國立國際關係學院短期訪問，同年底去莫斯科參加俄羅斯世界和平基金會的大會；2012年受邀到龍應台基金會演講，舉辦了第十八屆國際跨文化傳播學會的國際年會（18th IAICS-2012）；2012-2013年到美國喬治城大學短期研究訪問，客座主編了ICS國際期刊，到亞塞拜然（阿塞拜疆）首都巴庫參加了MGIMO-University的國際校友論壇大會，看見了母校校長和同學。總體而言，感受到了俄羅斯崛起與復甦的力量正在逐漸攀升。

　　對於俄羅斯的研究我本人多是抱持著一種興趣和想法，就是不斷反覆思考和總結俄羅斯，思考她的所作所為及其背後發生的原因和產生的現象。研究俄羅斯對於我的人生觀和影響應該來說是很深遠的。在感受到俄羅斯變化起起落落的同時，不斷又重新認識和了解俄羅斯，這樣對我總是能夠產生許多啟發和啟示。能夠堅持這條無用之路，主要還是要感謝我的先生吳非，他對於我工作和生活的犧牲奉獻和幫助支持。

在俄羅斯研究的推廣過程中，還要特別感謝中研院政治所吳玉山所長的支持，吳所長是國內研究列寧新經濟政策和蘇聯轉型的權威學者，同時吳所長給人的印象是溫文儒雅，是一位非常敦厚而嚴謹的學者，能受到吳所長的支持感覺是非常幸運的。同時要感謝台大人文高等研究院的黃俊傑院長，黃院長是我們國內通識教育的先行者，黃院長給了我去台大通識中心講授俄羅斯文化的機會，使得俄羅斯文化課程變成了是一門兼具專業和通識並且具有可傳播性的學科。還要感謝王定士教授，王定士教授對我而言是亦師亦友的前輩，向他請益總有非常愉快的感受和啟發。每次和這些先行者交流與請益時，總有令人非常讚嘆的感覺。在這裡還想要感謝林永芳所長和李細梅主任每年邀請我參加研討會，全國的俄羅斯研究者都會藉此齊聚一堂，感謝他們給我發表論文機會的同時也督促我不斷研究。

這次出書之前拜託了石之瑜教授作序，因為知道石老師是為學嚴謹但為人相當寬厚的人，他從事的全球漢學家——口述歷史計畫採訪了許多見證中俄關係歷史發展的人物，我很榮幸能夠參與他一小部分的工作。他多次隻身赴俄考察，令我們這些後學晚輩非常敬佩他的勇氣和氣魄，畢竟他是一句俄語都不會講的人。儘管如此，以他的學術知名度和影響力而言，他的親身參與所產生出的影響力卻是遠遠超過我們這些學習俄國語言和研究俄羅斯國情出身的人。在此表達對他對推動中俄關係研究和台俄學術交往貢獻的敬意。

最後，我想對我身處的元智大學表達誠摯的感謝，沒有元智大學提供的環境和條件，也很難完成自己的願望和想法。特此感謝張進福校長與前校長彭宗平教授；本部大家長王立文教授與孫長祥教授；人社院長劉阿榮教授以及謝登旺教授和王佳煌教授；陳興義研發長以及前任研發長孫一明教授和吳和生教授；國際處長余念一主任等人，感謝他們這幾年對我們從事學術活動與研究的鼓勵和支持。其中要特別感謝彭前校長和本部王部長的提攜和支持，是他們給予我各種想法和實踐最大的包容和忍耐。同時也要特別感謝幾位同仁的熱忱協助，是他們幫助我們促成了許多合作，包括林昭儀小姐、宋廣玲小姐、陳世娜小姐、范玉瑩小姐、謝桂香小姐以及江鴻津小姐等人，對於無法全部在此提及與疏漏了所有幫助過我們的朋友，在這裡要向他們表示深深的歉意。

　　匆匆執筆至次，已經感受到石之瑜教授日前新書發表會上的心情，他說每次出書之後總有一種反思的情緒，就是對自己的研究成果並不滿意。前輩尚且如此要求自己了，我想石老師對學術研究的追求和矜持是一種哲學式的思維，那種出自於自我挑戰和再戰高峰的熱忱和精神，同時也鼓勵著我們不斷向前邁進。再次感謝出版社的發行人宋政坤先生、邵亢虎主任編輯、林泰宏主任編輯與劉璞編輯等人的專業指正和熱忱協助。

　　在此後記中寥寥數句概括，不足和謬誤之處，尚祈各方先進惠予指正。

胡逢瑛

2013年6月1日於桃園內壢

Viewpoint 18　社會科學類　PF0113

俄羅斯再次崛起？
——雙頭鷹的亞太政策與戰略思想

作　　者／胡逢瑛
責任編輯／劉　璞
圖文排版／賴英珍
封面設計／陳佩蓉

發 行 人／宋政坤
法律顧問／毛國樑　律師
出版發行／秀威資訊科技股份有限公司
　　　　　114台北市內湖區瑞光路76巷65號1樓
　　　　　電話：+886-2-2796-3638　傳真：+886-2-2796-1377
　　　　　http://www.showwe.com.tw
劃撥帳號／19563868　戶名：秀威資訊科技股份有限公司
　　　　　讀者服務信箱：service@showwe.com.tw
展售門市／國家書店（松江門市）
　　　　　104台北市中山區松江路209號1樓
　　　　　電話：+886-2-2518-0207　傳真：+886-2-2518-0778
網路訂購／秀威網路書店：http://www.bodbooks.com.tw
　　　　　國家網路書店：http://www.govbooks.com.tw

2013年6月BOD一版
定價：250元
版權所有　翻印必究
本書如有缺頁、破損或裝訂錯誤，請寄回更換

國家圖書館出版品預行編目

俄羅斯再次崛起？:雙頭鷹的亞太政策與戰略思想 / 胡逢瑛
著. -- 一版. -- 臺北市 : 秀威資訊科技, 2013. 06
　　面; 　公分. -- (社會科學類 ; PF0113) (Viewpoint ;
18)
　BOD版
　ISBN 978-986-326-115-5 (平裝)

　1. 政治 2. 戰略思想 3. 俄國

574.48　　　　　　　　　　　　　　　102008944

讀者回函卡

感謝您購買本書，為提升服務品質，請填妥以下資料，將讀者回函卡直接寄回或傳真本公司，收到您的寶貴意見後，我們會收藏記錄及檢討，謝謝！如您需要了解本公司最新出版書目、購書優惠或企劃活動，歡迎您上網查詢或下載相關資料：http:// www.showwe.com.tw

您購買的書名：_____

出生日期：_____年_____月_____日

學歷：□高中 (含) 以下　　□大專　　□研究所 (含) 以上

職業：□製造業　□金融業　□資訊業　□軍警　□傳播業　□自由業
　　　□服務業　□公務員　□教職　　□學生　□家管　□其它_____

購書地點：□網路書店　□實體書店　□書展　□郵購　□贈閱　□其他

您從何得知本書的消息？

　□網路書店　□實體書店　□網路搜尋　□電子報　□書訊　□雜誌
　□傳播媒體　□親友推薦　□網站推薦　□部落格　□其他_____

您對本書的評價：(請填代號　1.非常滿意　2.滿意　3.尚可　4.再改進)

　封面設計____　版面編排____　內容____　文／譯筆____　價格____

讀完書後您覺得：

　□很有收穫　□有收穫　□收穫不多　□沒收穫

對我們的建議：_____

_____

_____

_____

11466
台北市內湖區瑞光路 76 巷 65 號 1 樓

秀威資訊科技股份有限公司　　收

BOD 數位出版事業部

....

（請沿線對折寄回，謝謝！）

姓　　名：＿＿＿＿＿＿＿＿＿　年齡：＿＿＿＿　性別：□女　□男

郵遞區號：□□□□□

地　　址：＿＿＿＿＿＿＿＿＿＿＿＿＿＿＿＿＿＿＿

聯絡電話：(日) ＿＿＿＿＿＿＿＿　(夜) ＿＿＿＿＿＿＿＿＿

E-mail：＿＿＿＿＿＿＿＿＿＿＿＿＿＿＿＿＿＿＿